FINANCIAL ASTROLOGY ALMANAC 2020

Trading & Investing Using the Planets

M.G. Bucholtz, B.Sc, MBA

Financial Astrology Almanac 2020 – Trading & Investing Using the Planets

For information contact the authior at: supercyclereport@gmail.com

Published by :
Wood Dragon Books,
Box 429, Mossbank, Saskatchewan, Canada, S0H 3G0
http://www.wooddragonbooks.com

ISBN: 978-1-989078-21-1

DEDICATION

To the many traders and investors who at some visceral level suspect there is more to the financial market system than P/E ratios and analyst recommendations.

You are correct. There is more. Much more. The markets are rooted in astronomical and astrological timing. This book will add a whole new dimension to your market activities.

DISCLAIMER

All material provided herein is based on material gleaned from mathematical and astrological publications researched by the author to supplement his own trading. This publication is written with sincere intent for those who actively trade and invest in the financial markets and who are looking to incorporate astrological phenomena and esoteric math into their market activity. While the material presented herein has proven reliable to the author in his personal trading and investing activity, there is no guarantee this material will continue to be reliable into the future.

The author and publisher assume no liability whatsoever for any investment or trading decisions made by readers of this book. The reader alone is responsible for all trading and investment outcomes and is further advised not to exceed his or her risk tolerances when trading or investing on the financial markets.

CONTENTS

Introduction

Many traders and investors think company press releases, media news opinions, quarterly earnings reports, and analyst targets drive stock prices and major index movements.

I disagree with this reasoning. There is something else that drives the financial markets. There is something else that creates the swing turning points on price charts. I have two opinions on what this something else might be.

My first opinion is that the financial markets are a reflection of the mass psychological emotion of traders, investors, and fund managers. Human emotion drives buying and selling decisions in the financial markets. When market participants are feeling positive, they are driven to buy. When they are feeling uncertain or negative, they are driven to sell.

Probing this idea deeper immediately yields the complex question - what drives human emotion?

Medical researchers have not definitively answered this question, but some say changes in blood alkalinity or acidity impact our emotions. Researcher Alireza Farnham at Tabriz University in Iran notes in a 2014 paper that cells in the human body generally require a pH of 7.4 for optimal performance. Bodily reactions to stimulating events can cause changes to cell pH and thereby affect our cognitive abilities and response activity.

Other academics state changes in chemical hormones in the bloodstream drive emotion. New York University brain researcher Joseph Ledoux notes in a 2012 paper a stimulating event sends a signal to the amygdala portion of the human brain which in turn sends a signal to the brain's central nucleus where defensive reactions and hormonal releases are formulated. Researchers Wirth and Gaffey, writing in the book *Handbook of Cognition and Emotion*, describe that hormones are chemicals produced in the hypothalamus and pituitary glands at the base of the brain. The brain responds to stimuli by sending a signal to the hypothalamus which in turn regulates the production of hormones which in turn provide a feedback loop to the brain which affects our emotion, cognition, and behaviour.

I am of the opinion that emotion also involves a nuance seldom discussed by academia. This nuance involves the ever-changing configurations of orbiting planets and other celestial bodies in our cosmos which influences our brain and body chemistry and thereby drives human emotion.

This opinion has been shaped by the many astrology publications I have studied including Tony Waterfall's insightful article from the *Spring 2014 NCGR Research Journal*. In his article Waterfall reminds readers that the Sun is the centre of our planetary system. The Sun emits massive amounts of solar radiation in all directions into the vastness of space. This radiation is called solar wind. This solar wind interacts with the magnetic fields around Mercury, Venus, Moon, Mars, Jupiter, Saturn, Uranus, Neptune, and Pluto. These planets accept and then disburse the solar wind radiation. As the radiation is disbursed, a goodly amount of it finds its way towards the magnetic field around planet Earth.

Changes in the density and speed of solar wind mean that the amount of radiation reaching Earth's magnetic field on a daily, weekly, or monthly basis will be ever-changing. As a result, the intensity of the Earth's magnetic field is also constantly changing. The alignment of the orbiting planets at any given time plays a key role in determining how much solar radiation is deflected towards Earth's magnetic field.

A simplistic way of viewing this entire arrangement is to think of a billiards table as the cosmos. The various balls on the table are the planets and other celestial bodies. The solar radiation is the white cue ball bouncing and deflecting off other balls on the table. The human body is largely comprised of water and we all have an electrical field that runs through our tissues. Therefore, basic physics demands that changes to the Earth's magnetic field will induce subtle changes to our bodily electric circuitry. These subtle electric changes are what drive our emotional responses.

Scientists and psychologists who are on a quest to learn more have come to call the developing science of how the cosmos affects humans, *cosmo-biology*. Ancient civilizations as far back as the Babylonians recognized cosmo-biology, but in a more rudimentary form. Their high priests tracked and recorded changes in the emotions of the people. These diviners and seers also tracked events, both fortuitous and disastrous. Although they lacked the ability to comprehend the physics of solar wind and magnetic fields, they were able to visually spot the planets Mercury, Venus, Mars, Jupiter, and Saturn in the heavens. They correlated changes in human emotion and changes in societal events to these planets.

They assigned to these planets the names of the various deities revered by the people. They identified and named various star constellations in the heavens and divided the heavens into twelve signs. This was the birth of *astrology* as we know it today.

My second opinion on what drives financial markets is even more brazen. I think the markets are manipulated from deep within New York, London, and other financial centers. This manipulation, based around astrological cycles and occurrences, creates the various swing highs and lows we see on stock charts. It is quite possible that once efforts to "swing" the markets are underway by these various parties, human emotion is stimulated by media frenzy thus providing a neural feedback loop which further stimulates the bodily emotion discussed by Farnham, Ledoux and others.

Starting in the early 1900s, esoteric thinkers such as the famous Wall Street trader W.D. Gann noted that basic astrology bore a striking correlation to changes on the financial markets. This was the birth of *Financial Astrology*. Gann based his writings and forecasts in part on the synodic cycles between various planets. He also delved deep into esoteric math, notably square root math and the concept of price squaring with time. He is well remembered for Gann Lines and the Square of Nine, techniques based on square root math. But Gann lived in a challenging time. Statute laws in New York state expressly forbade the use of occult science in business ventures. Gann therefore carefully concealed the basis for his market forecasts. Today many traders and investors attempt to emulate Gann but they do so in a linear fashion, looking for repetitive cycles on the calendar. What they are missing is the astrology component, which is anything but linear.

In the 1930s, Louise McWhirter contributed significantly to financial astrology. She identified an 18.6-year cyclical correlation between the general state of the American economy and the position of the North Node of the Moon. Her methodology extended to include the transiting Moon passing by key points of the 1792 natal birth horoscope of the New York Stock Exchange. She also identified a correlation between price movement of a stock and those times when transiting Sun, Mars, Jupiter and Saturn made hard aspects to the natal Sun position in the stock's natal birth (first trade) horoscope.

The late 1940s saw further advancements in the field of Financial Astrology when astrologer Garth Allen (a.k.a. Donald Bradley) produced his *Siderograph Model*. This complex model is based on aspects between the various transiting planets. Each aspect as it occurs is given a sinusoidal weighting as the orb (separation) between the planets varies. Bradley's model is as powerful today as it was in the late 1940s.

As you read these words, I invite you to think back to the dark days of late 2008 when there was genuine concern over the very survival of the financial market system. This timeframe was the end of an 18.6-year cycle of the North Node traveling around the zodiac. To those players at high levels in the financial system who understand astrology, this period was a prime opportunity to feast off the fear of the investing public and off the fear of government officials who were standing at the ready with lucrative bailout packages.

Think back to August 2015 and the market selloff that apparently no one saw coming. The reality is that this selloff started at a confluence of two events: August 2015 marked a Venus retrograde event. August 2015 also marked the appearance of Venus as a morning star after having been only visible as an evening star for the previous 263 days.

What about the early days of 2016 when Mercury was retrograde and the markets hit a rough patch? What about the weakness of June 2016 when Venus emerged from conjunction to become visible as an Evening Star?

How how about the dire predictions for financial market calamity following the election of Donald Trump to the White House? When the markets instead powered higher, analysts were flummoxed. Venus was making its declination minima right at the time of the US election. Venus declination minima events bear a striking correlation to changes of trend on US equity markets.

What about the early days of 2018 when fear once again gripped the system? Venus was at its declination minimum. Markets reached a turning point in the first week of October 2018 which again was Venus at a declination low. Add in the fact that Venus turned retrograde at the same time and the fear starts to make sense. Markets sold off sharply in mid-December before starting to recover. Sun was conjunct Saturn at this time which correlates strongly to trend changes on equity markets. The North Node had also just changed zodiac signs, an event which too aligns to trend changes.

More recently, the markets hit a sudden rough patch in early August 2019. Mercury had just finished a retrograde event and the Federal Reserve cut interest rates as Moon transited a key point on the NYSE 1792 natal horoscope.

I personally began to embrace Financial Astrology in 2012 which was a monumental shift given that my educational background comprises an Engineering degree and an MBA degree. As I pen the text for this 2020 Almanac, I find myself again at school, this time in pursuit of a M.Sc. degree. Three linear-thinking, left-brain degrees to be certain. Since 2012, my research and back-testing has satisfied me that a correlation does indeed exist between astrology and the financial markets. This almanac represents my eleventh publication on the subject of Financial Astrology.

This almanac begins by offering the reader a look at the cyclical math and science of astrology. What then follows is an examination of the New York Stock Exchange for the twelve months of calendar year 2020. Each monthly examination presents a summation of key dates when astrology events pose a high probability of influencing market price action. For readers outside of North America, please note that in today's interconnected financial world, movements on the New York Exchange are often felt on other exchanges around the globe.

This almanac then provides a look at various commodity futures and the astro phenomena that influence their price action. I next provide a look at Gann Lines and the concept of Price Square Time, a powerful tool said to have been used by W.D. Gann. I go on to introduce the concept of Quantum Price Lines, a powerful esoteric technique that can be used when applying astrology to making trading and investing decisions. I further offer market insights based on planetary declinations and planetary cycles and end the almanac with an examination of the Shmitah and also Kabbalistic math as alternative ways of measuring time.

When applying astrology to trading and investing, it is vital at all times to be aware of the price trend. There are many ways of observing trend. My personal experience has shown me that the chart indicators developed by J. Welles Wilder are very effective at identifying trend changes. In particular, the DMI and the Volatility Stop are two indicators that should be taken seriously. As a trader and investor, look for a change of trend that aligns to an astrology event. When you see the trend change, you should take action. Whether that action is implementing a long position, a short position, an Options strategy, or just tightening up on a stop loss will depend on your personal appetite for risk and on your investment and trading objectives. Using astrology for financial investing is not about trying to take action at each and every astro event that comes along because not all astro events are powerful enough to induce a change of trend.

This Almanac is designed to be a resource for you to help you stay abreast of the various astro events that 2020 holds in store. I sincerely hope after you have applied the material in this almanac to your trading and investing activity, you will embrace Financial Astrology as a valuable tool.

To further set the tone for what you are about to read in this almanac, I leave you with the following quotes on the subject of astrology:

"An unfailing experience of mundane events in harmony with the changes occurring in the heavens, has instructed and compelled my unwilling belief." (Johannes Kepler, astronomer and mathematician 1571-1630)

"Heaven sends down its good and evil symbols and wise men act accordingly." (Confucius – Chinese philosopher 551-479 BC)

"The controls of life are structured as forms and nuclear arrangements, in relation with the motions of the universe." (Louis Pasteur-scientist 1822-1895)

"Oh the wonderful knowledge to be found in the stars. Even the smallest things are written there...if you had but skill to read." (Ben Franklin-one of the Founding Fathers of America 1706-1790)

"It's common knowledge that a large percentage of Wall Street brokers use Astrology." (Donald Reagan, formerly Ronald Reagan's Chief of Staff)

References

Farnam A. (2014). pH of soul: how does acid-base balance affect our cognition?, *BioImpacts*, 4(2), pp. 53–54.

LeDoux J. E. (2012). Evolution of human emotion: a view through fear. *Progress in Brain Research*, 195, pp. 431–442.

Wirth, M., Gaffey, E. (2014). Hormones and Emotion. *Handbook of Cognition and Emotion*. Eds: Robinson, Watkins and Harmon-Jones, pp. 69-94.

CHAPTER ONE

Fundamentals

Astronomy is the science pertaining to the positioning and motion of planetary bodies in our solar system. *Astrology* is an ancient quasi-science focused on the correlation between the planets, events of nature, and behaviour of mankind. This ancient quasi-science is rooted in thousands of years of empirical observation across many civilizations.

•   The ancient Sumerians, Akkadians and Babylonians between the 4th and 2nd centuries BCE believed the affairs of mankind could be gauged by watching the motions of certain stars and planets. They recorded their predictions and future indications of prosperity and calamity on clay tablets. These early recordings form the foundation of modern day astrology.

•   Ancient Egyptian artifacts show that high priests Petosiris and Necepso who lived during the reign of

Ramses II were revered for their knowledge of astrology. The Egyptian culture is thought to have developed a 12 month x 30 day time-keeping method based on the repeated appearances of constellations.

• Ancient Indian and Chinese artifacts reveal that astrology held an esteemed place in those societies for many thousands of years.

• Hipparchus, Pythagoras, and Plato are key names from the Greek era. Historians think Pythagoras assigned mathematical values to the relations between celestial bodies. Plato is thought to have offered up predictions relating celestial bodies to human fates. Hipparchus is thought to have compiled a star catalogue which popularized astrology.

• In the latter years of the Roman empire, astrology was used for political gain. Important military figures surrounded themselves with philosophers such as Ptolemy and Valens. In 126, Ptolemy penned four books describing the influence of the stars. His works are collectively called the *Tetrabiblos*. In 160, Valens penned *Anthologies* in which he further summarized the principles of astrology.

Following the conversion of Emperor Constantine to Christianity in 312, the use of astrology for gain became a crime according to the Church of Rome. Astrology began a slow retreat to the sidelines where, for the most part, it remains today. Despite having been sidelined by a Church seeking to protect its authority, astrology quietly continued to be used by leading thinkers of the day such as Galileo, Brahe, Nostradamus, Kepler, Bacon and Newton. Thanks to the tenacity of these men, astrology was prevented from fading away into a distant memory.

The Ecliptic and the Zodiac

The Sun is at the center of our solar system. The Earth, Moon, planets and various other asteroid bodies complete our planetary system. The various planets and other asteroid bodies rotate 360 degrees around the Sun following a path called the *ecliptic plane*. As shown in Figure 1, Earth (and its Equator) is slightly tilted (approximately 23.5 degrees) relative to the ecliptic plane. Projecting the Earth's equator into space produces the *celestial equator plane*. There are two points of intersection between the ecliptic plane and celestial equator plane. Mathematically, this makes sense as two non-parallel planes must intersect at two points. These points are commonly called the *vernal equinox* (occurring at March 20th) and the *autumnal equinox* (occurring at September 20th). You will recognize these dates as the first day of Spring and the first day of Fall, respectively. Dividing the ecliptic plane into twelve equal sections of 30 degrees results in what astrologers call the *zodiac*. The twelve portions of the zodiac have names including Aries, Cancer, Leo and so on. Ancient civilizations looking skyward identified patterns of stars called constellations that align to these twelve zodiac divisions. If these names sound familiar, they should. You routinely see all twelve names in the daily horoscope section of your morning newspaper.

The Glyphs

Figure 2 illustrates a zodiac wheel. In this wheel, you will notice that the twelve divisions of the ecliptic have each been assigned a peculiar looking symbol. These symbols are called *glyphs*.

The starting point or zero degree point of the zodiac wheel is the sign Aries, located at the vernal equinox of each year. The vernal equinox is when, from our vantage point on Earth, the Sun appears at zero degrees Aries. The autumnal equinox is when, from our vantage point on Earth, the Sun appears at 180 degrees from zero Aries (0 degrees of Libra).

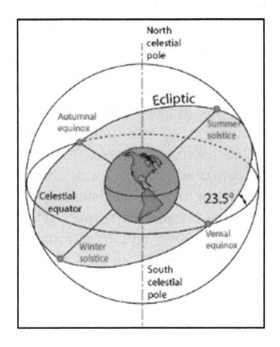

Figure 1
The Ecliptic

Figure 2
The Zodiac Wheel

The Celestial Bodies

In addition to the Sun and Moon, there are eight celestial bodies important to the application of astrology to trading and investing on the financial markets. These planets are Mercury, Venus, Mars, Jupiter, Saturn, Uranus, Neptune, and Pluto. Figure 3 illustrates these various bodies in orbit around the Sun on the ecliptic plane. Mercury is the closest to the Sun while Pluto is the farthest away.

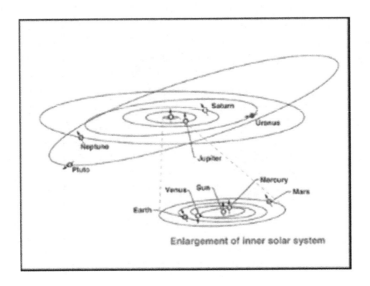

Enlargement of inner solar system

Figure 3

The Planets

These planets are also denoted by *glyphs*. Figure 4 presents these glyphs along with the zodiac sign glyphs.

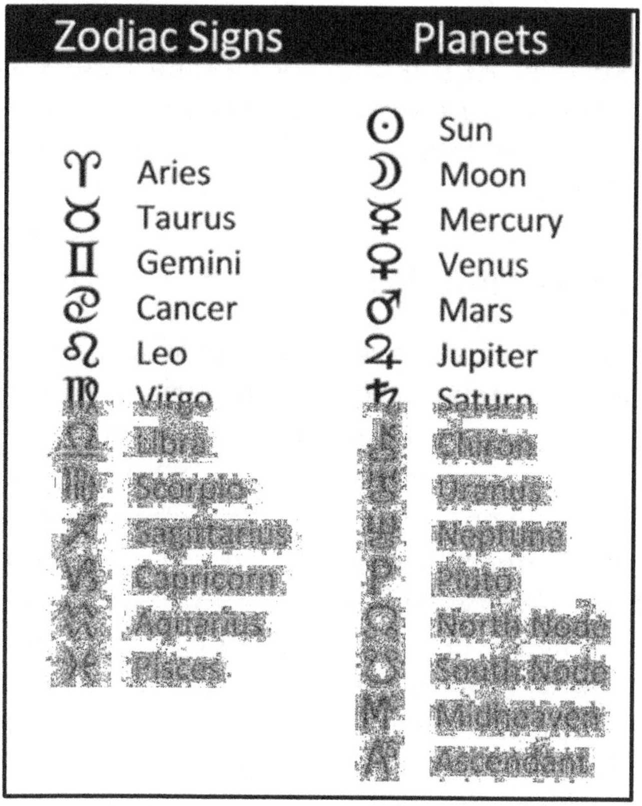

Zodiac Signs		Planets	
		☉	Sun
♈	Aries	☽	Moon
♉	Taurus	☿	Mercury
♊	Gemini	♀	Venus
♋	Cancer	♂	Mars
♌	Leo	♃	Jupiter
♍	Virgo	♄	Saturn
♎	Libra		Chiron
♏	Scorpio	♅	Uranus
♐	Sagittarius	♆	Neptune
♑	Capricorn	♇	Pluto
♒	Aquarius	☊	North Node
♓	Pisces	☋	South Node
		M	Midheaven
		A	Ascendant

Figure 4

The Glyphs

Declination

As the various celestial bodies make their respective journeys around the Sun, they can be seen to move above and below the celestial equator plane. This movement is termed *declination*. Celestial bodies experience declinations of up to about 25 degrees above and below the celestial equator plane.

Mercury, Venus, and Mars endure frequent changes in declination due to the gravitational force of the Sun. Planets like Jupiter, Saturn, Neptune, Uranus and Pluto also experience declination changes but these changes are slower to evolve. As this almanac will illustrate, changes in the declination of a celestial body can affect the financial markets. In particular, Venus and Mars have notable effects.

Parallel and Contra-Parallel

Declination can be viewed one planet at a time or by pairs of planets. Let's suppose that at a particular time Mars can be seen as being 10 degrees of declination above the celestial equator and at that same time Venus is also at 10 degrees of declination. Let's further suppose that we allow for up to 1.5 degrees tolerance in our measurement of declinations. We would say these two planets were at *parallel declination*. Let's take another example and suppose that at a given time Jupiter was at 5 degrees of declination above the celestial equator and at that same time period Pluto was at 6 degrees declination below the celestial equator. Again, let's allow for up to 1.5 degrees of tolerance. We would say that Jupiter and Pluto were at *contra-parallel declination*. As this Almanac will show, parallel and contra-parallel events can have an influence on the financial markets.

The Moon

Just as the planets orbit 360 degrees around the Sun, the Moon orbits 360 degrees around the Earth. The Moon orbits the Earth in a plane of motion called the *lunar orbit plane*. This plane is inclined at about 5 degrees to the ecliptic plane as the dotted line in Figure 5 shows. The Moon orbits Earth with a slightly elliptical pattern in approximately 27.3 days, relative to an observer located on a fixed frame of reference such as the Sun. This time period is known as a *sidereal month*. However, during one sidereal month, an observer located on Earth (a moving frame of reference) will revolve part way around the Sun. To that Earth-bound observer, a complete orbit of the Moon around the Earth will appear longer than the sidereal month at approximately 29.5 days. This 29.5 day period of time is known as a *synodic month* or more commonly a lunar month. The lunar month plays a key role in applying astrology to the financial markets as will be detailed throughout this book.

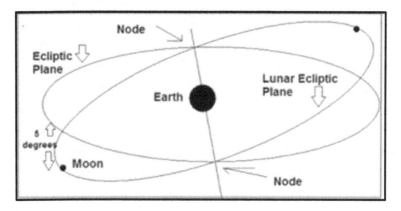

Figure 5

The Nodes

The Moon figures prominently in the history and lore of astrology. Throughout the centuries, the Moon has been associated with health, mood, and dreams. In 6th century Constantinople (modern day Istanbul, Turkey), physicians at the court of Emperor Justinian advised that gout could be cured by inscribing verses of Homer on a copper plate when the Moon was in the sign of Libra or Leo. In 17th century France, astrologers used the Moon to explain mood changes in women. In 17th century England, herbal remedy practitioners advised people to pluck the petals of the peony flower when the Moon was waning. During the Renaissance period, it was thought that dreams could come true if the Moon was in the signs of Taurus, Leo, Aquarius, or Scorpio.

Today, we do not wait for dreams to come true according to the Moon. But, the Moon nonetheless continues to be recognized as a powerful celestial body. Just as the gravitational pull of the Moon can influence the action of ocean tides, this same pull somehow also influences our emotions of fear and hope. As our emotions of fear and hope change, our investment buying and selling decisions also change. These emotional changes correlate to changes in price trend action. When this correlation is overlaid with technical chart analysis, a whole new dimension in trading and investing opens up as this almanac will detail.

The Nodes

Another mathematical construct central to Financial Astrology is the *Nodes*. The Nodes are the points of intersection between the ecliptic plane and the Moon's ecliptic plane. Figure 5 also illustrates the Nodes. In astrology, typically only the North Node is referred to. The importance of the North Node will be emphasized later in this almanac when the *McWhirter Method* is discussed.

Eclipses

A *solar eclipse* occurs when the Moon passes through a Node during a New Moon event. A *lunar eclipse* occurs when the Moon passes through a Node during a Full Moon event.

As observed from the Earth, a solar eclipse occurs when the Moon passes in front of the Sun. The type of solar eclipse event depends on the distance of the Moon from the Earth during the event. A total solar eclipse occurs when the Earth is completely blanketed by Moon's shadow. Annular and partial eclipses occur when the Earth is only partially blanketed by the Moon's shadow.

Lunar eclipses occur when the Moon is on the far side of the Earth from the Sun. Lunar eclipses only occur at a Full Moon event.

Ascendant, Descendant, MC and IC

As the Earth rotates on its axis once in every 24 hours, an observer situated on Earth will detect an apparent motion of the constellation stars that define the zodiac. To better define this motion, astrologers apply four cardinal points to the zodiac, almost like the north, south, east and west points on a compass. These cardinal points divide the zodiac into four quadrants. The east point is termed the *Ascendant* and is often abbreviated Asc. The west point is termed the *Descendant* and is often abbreviated Dsc. The south point is termed the *Mid-Heaven* (from the Latin Medium Coeli) and is often abbreviated MC or MH. The north point is termed the *Imum Coeli* (Latin for bottom of the sky) and is abbreviated IC. Figure 6 illustrates the placement of these cardinal points on a typical zodiac wheel. The importance of the Ascendant and Mid-Heaven will be emphasized later in this almanac when the McWhirter Method is discussed.

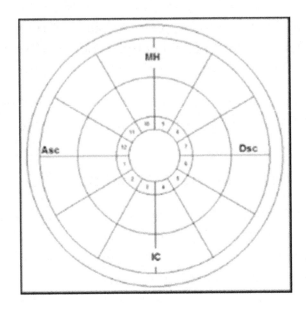

Figure 6

Cardinal Points

Geocentric and Heliocentric Astrology

Astrology comes in two distinct varieties – geocentric and heliocentric.

In *geocentric astrology*, the Earth is the vantage point for observing the planets as they pass through the signs of the zodiac. Owing to the different times for the planets to each orbit the Sun, an astrologer situated on Earth would see the planets making distinct angles (called aspects) with one another and also with the Sun. The aspects that are commonly used in Astrology are 0, 30, 45, 60, 90, 120, 150 and 180 degrees. In Financial Astrology, it is common to refer to only the 0, 90, 120 and 180 degree aspects.

In *heliocentric astrology*, the Sun is the vantage point for observing the planets as they pass through the signs of the zodiac. An observer positioned on the Sun would also see the orbiting planets making aspects with one another.

To identify these aspects, astrologers use *Ephemeris Tables*. For geocentric astrology, the *New American Ephemeris for the 21st Century* is commonly used. It is available at most bookstores. For heliocentric astrology, the *American Heliocentric Ephemeris* is a good resource.

For faster aspect determination, two excellent software programs available are *Millenium Trax* produced by AIR Software and *Solar Fire Gold* produced by software company Astrolabe. My preference is the Solar Fire Gold product. I also use a market platform called *Market Analyst*. This brilliant piece of software, originally developed in Australia, allows the user to generate end of day price charts for equities and commodities from a multitude of exchanges and then overlay various astrological aspects and occurrences onto the chart. As your journey into astrology deepens, you might be tempted to spend the money to acquire this software program.

Synodic and Sidereal

The vantage point of either Earth or Sun then leads to two more concepts, *synodic* and *sidereal*. These descriptors were used in the context of the Moon, as discussed earlier in this section. These terms apply to the other planets as well. To an earth-bound observer, a synodic time period is the time between two successive occurrences. That is, how many days does it take for Sun passing Pluto on the zodiac wheel to again pass Pluto? To a Sun-bound observer, a sidereal time period is the number of days (or years) it takes for a planet to orbit the Sun. These time frames play roles in assessing market cycles as will be discussed in this almanac. Figure 7 presents synodic and sidereal data.

Planet	Synodic Period	Sidereal Period
Mercury	116 days	88 days
Venus	584 days	225 days
Mars	780 days	1.9 years
Jupiter	399 days	11.9 years
Saturn	378 days	29.5 years
Uranus	370 days	84 years
Neptune	368 days	164.8 years
Pluto	367 days	248.5 years

Figure 7

Synodic and Sidereal Data

Retrograde

Think of the planets orbiting the Sun as a group of cars travelling around a racetrack. Consider what happens as a fast moving car approaches a slower moving car from behind. At first, all appears normal. An observer in the fast moving car sees the slower moving car heading in the same direction. Gradually, the observer in the fast car sees that he will soon overtake the slow car. For a brief moment in time as the fast car overtakes the slower car the observer in the fast car notices that the slower car appears to stand still and even move backwards. Of course the slow car is not really standing still. This is simply an optical illusion.

These brief illusory periods are what astrologers call *retrograde* events. To ancient societies, retrograde events were of great significance as human emotion was often seen to be changeable at these events. Is it possible that our DNA is hard-wired such that we feel uncomfortable at retrograde events?

From the vantage point of an observer on Earth, there will be three or four times during a year when Earth and Mercury pass by each other on this celestial racetrack. There will be one or perhaps two times per year when Earth and Venus pass each other. There will be one time every two years when Earth and Mars pass each other.

Elongation and Conjunction

From an observer's vantage point on Earth, there will also be times when planets are seen to be at maximum angles of separation from the Sun. These events are what astronomers refer to as *maximum easterly* and *maximum westerly* elongations. These events do have a correlation to times of trend change on markets.

Mercury and Venus are closer to the Sun than is the Earth. From our vantage point on Earth, there will be times when Mercury and Venus are between the Earth and the Sun. Likewise, there will be times when the Sun is between the Earth and Mercury or Venus. On the zodiac wheel, the times when Mercury or Venus are in the same zodiac sign and degree as the Earth are what astronomers call *conjunctions*.

An *Inferior Conjunction* occurs when Mercury or Venus is between Earth and the Sun. A *Superior Conjunction* occurs when the Sun is between Earth and Mercury or Venus. Figure 8 illustrates the concept of elongation and conjunction.

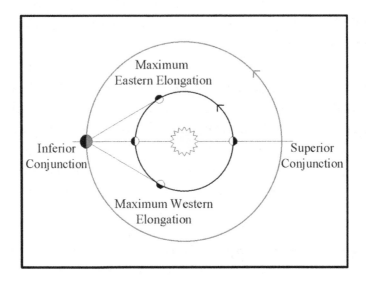

Figure 8
Superior and Inferior Conjunction

Conjunction events are closely related to retrograde events in that they occur on either side of retrograde events. For example, in 2018 Venus was retrograde from October 5 to November 15. Its actual Inferior Conjunction was recorded on October 26.

After Venus has been at Inferior Conjunction, it will be visible as a Morning Star. After it has been at Superior Conjunction it will be visible as an Evening Star. Venus was at Superior Conjunction on March 28, 2013 (8 Aries), October 25, 2014 (1 Scorpio), June 6, 2016 (16 Gemini), and January 8, 2018 (18 Capricorn). Venus was at Inferior Conjunction on June 6, 2012 (15 Gemini), January 11, 2014 (21 Capricorn), August 15, 2015 (22 Leo), March 25, 2017 (4 Aries), and October 26, 2018 (3 Scorpio). Plot these groups of Superior Conjunction events on a zodiac wheel. Note how they can be joined to form a 5-pointed star called a *pentagram*. Likewise, the Inferior Conjunction events can be plotted and joined to form a pentagram. Such is the elegance and mystique of the cosmos.

With these fundamentals now provided for you, it is time to apply them to the financial markets by way of example. The chapters that follow contain example charts to illustrate the various astro phenomena along with 2020 dates of when various astro events will occur.

CHAPTER TWO

The Master Cycle

The venerable W.D. Gann closely followed the cycles of Jupiter and Saturn.

To an observer situated on a fixed vantage point such as the Sun, Jupiter would be seen orbiting the Sun in about 12 years and Saturn in just over 29 years. But, Gann took these orbital cycles one step further and noted that every 20 or so years Jupiter and Saturn were at conjunction, separated by zero degrees. This is what he called the *Master Cycle.*

Gann further noted that the financial markets seemed to be affected by this Master Cycle. The market crash of 1901 aligned to a conjunction of these two outer planets. In 1920, the U.S. economy encountered a recession and in 1921 the financial markets reached a low point, again at the conjunction of these two heavy-weight planets. In 1941, the markets recorded a low point a couple months after another Jupiter-Saturn conjunction. The early-1960s should have seen another major turning point at the end of a Master Cycle. There was a drawdown in the U.S. equity markets that historians now call the Kennedy Slide, but it did not align perfectly to the Master Cycle. As it turns out, this one exception the Master Cycle was affected by something far more powerful. This powerful event was a *Cardinal Cross*. Picture a rectangle with its parallel sides and parallel ends. Now, place this rectangle inside of the zodiac. The corner points of the rectangle are pairs of planets. This 1965 Cardinal Cross involved eight celestial bodies (Neptune was the odd man out). With the Dow Jones Average at near 8000 points, the Cardinal Cross marked a significant turning point for the US equity market. It would not be until 1995 when the US equity market would again test this 8000 level.

In the Spring of 1981, Jupiter and Saturn recorded a Master Cycle conjunct event. A handful of months later, the U.S. equity markets recorded a very important low that marked the onset of a massive bull market that ran until the next conjunction event in mid-2000. If you were active in the markerts then, the tech-bubble probably brings back painful memories of money lost in your brokerage account. Figure 9 illustrates how the S&P 500 was making its peak as Jupiter and Saturn were making their conjunction.

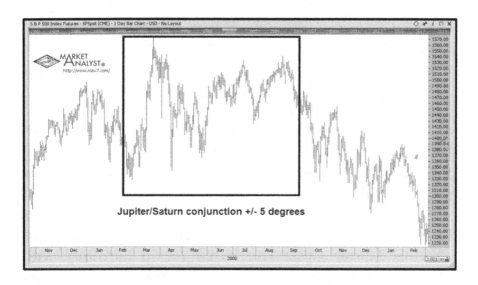

Figure 9
Jupiter / Saturn Conjunction in 2000

We are now within eyesight of the next conjunction event which will arrive in the middle of 2020, leading up to the U.S. Presidential election. For many traders and investors, I think 2020 has potential to leave lasting memories. This conjunction event could be a powerful one as the zodiac chart shows 8 celestial features crammed into a 90 degree segment of the chart. That is a lot of concentrated planetary energy. The time to start strategizing for this event is right now if you wish to avoid damage to your investment account as was the case in 2000 at the last Master Cycle event.

This coming Master Cycle event will be a crucial test of the voracity of astrology. In 2019 we saw the outspoken PresidentTrump pressure the Federal Reserve into cutting interest rates when a cut was deemed by many to have been un-necessary. Will the Federal Reserve act irrationaly to stem any market weakness brought on by this Master Cycle? Will any Master Cycle weakness even have a chance to gain momentum? In my view, the markets are overdue for a good cleansing of sorts. Valuations are stretched too thin and good money is chasing bad opportunities creating bubbles. A classic example from 2019 was the marijuana sector which became over-hyped and over-inflated by players seeking short term gains. This entire sector sector has now collapsed on itself.

I sincerely hope that the Federal Reserve stands down and lets this Master Cycle run its course in harmony with science and Nature. The hot, bubbly air needs to be let from the markets. Make use of stop losses if during 2020 the markets begin to ease off. At all times maintain perspective. Don't let the media warning of gloom and doom throw you. Use the end of this Master Cycle as a possible buying opportunity.

CHAPTER THREE

The 18.6 Year Cycle

There exists another longer cycle that more people ought to be more aware of. This cycle was first written about in the 1930s by a mysterious figure called Louise McWhirter. I say *mysterious* because in all my research travels I have not come across any other writings by her nor have I found much reference to her in other manuscripts. I am almost of the opinion that the name was a pseudonym for someone seeking to disseminate astrological ideas while remaining anonymous.

McWhirter recognized that the transit of the North Node of the Moon around the zodiac wheel takes 18.6 years and that the Node progresses in a backwards motion through the zodiac signs. Recall from the Fundamentals chapter earlier in this text that the Moon orbits the Earth in a plane of motion called the Lunar Ecliptic. Two planes that are not parallel will always intersect at two points. The two points where the Lunar Ecliptic intersects that plane of motion of planet Earth are termed the North Node and South Node.

Through examination of copious amounts of economic data provided by Leonard P. Ayers of the Cleveland Trust Company, McWhirter was able to conclude that when the North Node moves through certain zodiac signs, the economic business cycle reaches a low point and when the Node is in certain other signs, the business cycle is at its strongest. This line of thinking is still with us today. The most notable authority who embraces this cycle is Australian economist Fred Harrison. In his published work, he discusses this long economic cycle going back to the Industrial Revolution. But, to maintain respect in academic circles, he stops just shy of stating a connection to astrology.

In particular, McWhirter was able to discern the following:

• As the Node enters Aquarius, the low point of economic activity has been reached.
• As the Node leaves Aquarius and begins to transit through Capricorn and Sagittarius, the economy starts to return to normal.
• As the Node passes through Scorpio and Libra, the economy is functioning above normal.
• As the Node transits through Leo, the high point in economic activity has been reached.
• As the Node transits through Cancer and Gemini, the economy is easing back towards normal.
• As the Node enters the sign of Taurus, the economy begins to slow.
• As the Node enters Aquarius, the low point of economic activity has been reached and a full 18.6 year cycle has been completed.

McWhirter further observed some secondary factors that could influence the tenor of economic activity in a good way, no matter which sign the Node was in at the time:

- Jupiter being 0 degrees conjunct to the Node
- Jupiter being in Gemini or Cancer
- Pluto being at a favorable aspect to the Node

McWhirter also observed some secondary factors that can influence the tenor of economic activity in a bad way, no matter which sign the Node was in at the time:

- Saturn being 0, 90 or 180 degrees to the Node
- Saturn in Gemini or Cancer
- Uranus in Gemini
- Uranus being 0, 90 or 180 degrees to the Node
- Pluto being at an unfavorable aspect to the Node

So, what does 2020 portend? In the Summer of 2019, there were rumblings about an imminent recession. But, then some large investment banking firms in New York weighed in with a more extended opinion. Soon the media was talking about a recession at some later point in 2020 or 2021. To me, this is evidence that the large money firms in New York are paying close attention to the 18.6-year cycle.

North Node will be in the sign of Cancer in early 2020. By late 2020, the Node will be mid-way through Gemini. McWhirter's work suggests this movement through Cancer and Gemini will align to a slowing of the economy back toward normal levels of activity. What is missing from this Node consideration for 2020 are any of the negative aspects of Saturn, Uranus or Pluto to the Node. If each of us looks around in our communities, I think we can all agree that economic activity is easing. But, we are not quite ready for a full blown recession yet.

Recession will manifest in a big way starting in late 2024. By 2026 the Node will be in Aquarius to mark the end of the 18.6 year cycle and very likely another financial crisis. Uranus at the time will be in Gemini and Saturn will be 90 degrees to the Node. These astro positions warn of a very negative time. One other astro cycle that I follow is even indicating the U.S.A. being at war at the time the 18.6 year cycle ends. But these events are still six years distant, so try not to worry too much. Just be aware. Plan accordingly.

There are a couple other astro events that should be watched along with the McWhirter cycle. These events involve aspects of the Sun to Jupiter and Sun to Saturn. In late December 2019, Sun and Jupiter will make a zero degree conjunction. A couple weeks later in mid-January 2020 Sun and Saturn will be conjunct. These powerful conjunctions all too often align to trend changes or intensification of trend on the US equity complex. Whether the trend changes to the upside or to the downside come early 2020, ongoing propensity for trade disputes with China and associated tariff impositions will certainly not benefit matters. Nor will ongoing Presidential impeachment efforts.

CHAPTER FOUR

Venus Cycles 2020

Venus orbits the Sun in 225 days relative to an observer standing at a fixed venue like the Sun. To an observer here on Earth, a moving frame of reference, Venus appears to take 584 days to orbit the Sun. Along the way, that same observer on Earth will note periods of time when Venus is not visible in the early morning or evening sky. This is because the planet is between Earth and Sun in its orbital journey. This is the Inferior Conjunction. As Venus slowly moves out of this conjunction, it will become visible as the Morning Star. During that part of its journey when Venus is 180 degrees opposite Earth, it is said to be at Superior Conjunction. As it moves out of this conjunction, it becomes visible as the Evening Star.

Venus was at Superior Conjunction on March 28, 2013 (8 Aries), October 25, 2014 (1 Scorpio), June 6, 2016 (16 Gemini) and January 8, 2018 (18 Capricorn). Venus was at

Inferior Conjunction on June 6, 2012 (15 Gemini), January 11, 2014 (21 Capricorn), August 15, 2015 (22 Leo), March 25, 2017 (4 Aries), and October 26, 2018 (3 Scorpio). Plot these groups of Superior Conjunction events on a zodiac wheel. Note how they can be joined to form a 5-pointed star called a pentagram. Likewise, the Inferior Conjunction events can be plotted and joined to form a pentagram.

As Venus orbits around the Sun along the ecliptic plane, it moves above and below the plane. The high points and low points made during this travel are termed *declination maxima and minima*. In early 2018, a Venus Superior Conjunction and declination minimum was followed closely by a steep 300 point sell-off on the S&P 500. A significant trend change immediately preceded an Inferior Conjunction and declination minimum in October 2018. This was followed by an acceleration of trend to the downside. As the chart in Figure 10 illustrates, in July 2019 talk of an imminemt recession and talk of an impasse with China over trade disputes caused a sharp sell-off on the S&P 500. But, notice that this event was nothing more than a Venus Superior Conjunction combined with a Venus declination maximum. As 2019 winds to a close, the White House continues to work towards a phase-one partial resolution to the trade dispute with China. The equity market generally anticipates a resolution. But, a Venus Superior Conjunction is set to occur into early December, 2019. A short, adverse reaction would not be out of the question.

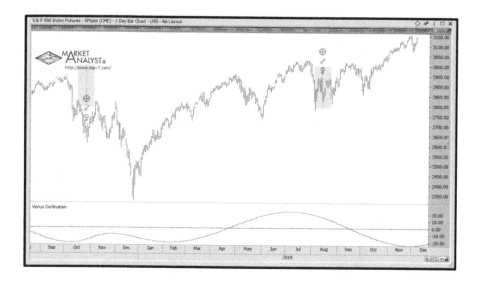

Figure 10
Venus Conjunction and Declination

As these conjunctions and declination events approach, it is highly advisable to be alert for sudden market moves that could affect your investment portfolio. For 2020, Venus will make a declination maximum in early May and will be on its way to a declination minimum in late December.

There will be an Inferior Conjunction on June 3. Watch for adverse market moves on either side of this date. There are no Superior Conjunctions of Venus until March of 2021.

Another cyclical event pertaining to Venus is retrograde. When discussing the basics of astrology in a previous chapter, I used the analogy of cars on a racetrack passing each other to explain retrograde. To help understand the science of Venus retrograde, consider the diagram in Figure 11.

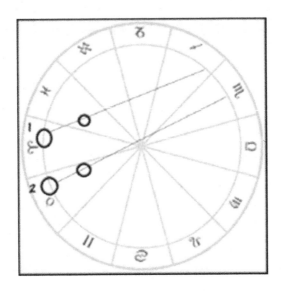

Figure 11
Venus retrograde – the concept

In 30 days of time planet Earth (shown as the larger circles in the diagram) will travel 30 degrees of the zodiac (from point 1 to point 2). But, Venus is a faster mover. In the same 30 days of time, Venus (shown as the smaller circles) will travel through about 42 degrees of the zodiac, passing by Earth in the process. From our vantage point here on Earth, initially as Venus is setting up to pass Earth, we see Venus in the sign of Sagittarius. These sign determinations are made in Figure 11 by extending a line from planet Earth through Venus to the outer edge of the zodiac wheel. As Venus completes its trip past Earth, we see it in the sign of Scorpio. In other words, the way we see it here on Earth, Venus has moved backwards as it passed Earth. This is the concept of retrograde. To the ancients who did not fully understand how the cosmos worked, it must have been awe-inspiring to see a planet move backwards in the heavens relative to the constellation stars.

There is a curiously strong correlation between equity

markets and Venus retrograde. Sometimes Venus retrograde events encompass a sharp market inflection point. Sometimes a market peak or bottom will follow closely behind a retrograde event. Sometimes a peak or bottom will immediately precede a retrograde event. When you know a Venus retrograde event is approaching, use a suitable chart technical indicator such as DMI or Wilder Volatility Stop to determine if the price trend is changing.

Figure 12 illustrates price behavior of the S&P 500 Index during 2018.

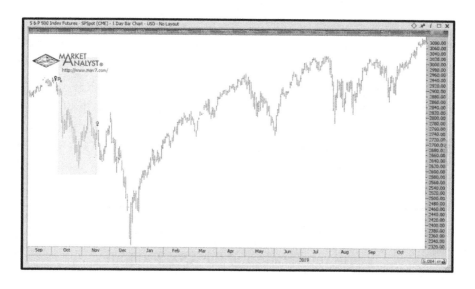

Figure 12
S&P 500 Index and Venus retrograde

Note the tight correlation between the trend change and the onset of retrograde. The event illustrated in this Figure meant a 300 point loss on the S&P 500. Not all Venus retrograde events are so severe. A retrograde event in March, 2017 saw only a 50 point loss. Knowing that the potential exists for sizeable moves, aggressive traders can avail themselves of these retrograde correlations. Less aggressive investors may simply wish to place a stop loss order under their positions to guard against sharp price pullbacks.

As a further example, Figure 13 illustrates price performance of the S&P/ASX All Australian 200 Index. Venus retrograde events in 2017 and 2018 have been overlaid.

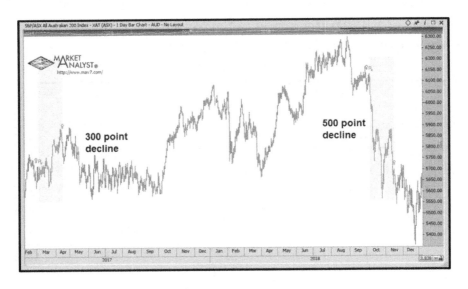

Figure 13
Venus retrograde and the ASX 200 Index

For 2020, Venus will be retrograde from May 13 through June 24. If the Gann Master Cycle is to negatively impact the markets, I would not be at all surprised to see the impact stat to manifext itself at this retrograde event.

CHAPTER FIVE

Mercury Cycles 2020

Mercury is the smallest planet in our solar system. Mercury is also the closest planet to the Sun. As a result of its proximity to the powerful gravitational pull of the Sun, Mercury moves very quickly – completing one sidereal orbit of the Sun in 88 days.

Scientists at NASA have now concluded that Mercury does in fact have a di-polar magnetic field. This field is strong enough to deflect solar wind particles that have emanated from the Sun. These deflected solar winds then carry on towards the Earth. Scientists have also determined that Mercury has an eccentric orbit in which its distance from the Sun will range from 46 million kms to 70 million kms. When Mercury is nearer to the Sun (ie 46 million kms away), it is moving at its fastest (~56.6 kms per second). When Mercury is farther from the Sun (ie 70 million kms away), it is moving slower (~38.7 kms per second). Related to Mercury's orbit is its elongation. As discussed earlier in this almanac, elongation refers to the angle between a planet and the Sun, using Earth as a reference point. Figure 14 illustrates the notion of elongation.

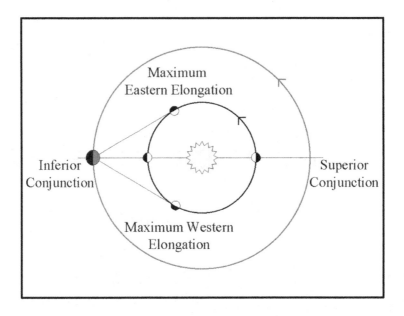

Figure 14
Elongation of Mercury

In 2018 Mercury was at its greatest easterly elongation on March 15, July 12 and November 6. Mercury was at its greatest westerly elongation on January 1, April 29, August 26 and December 15.

For 2019, Mercury was at its greatest easterly elongation February 27, June 23 and October 23. It was at its greatest westerly elongation April 11, August 9 and November 28.

Figure 15 illustrates some of these 2019 events on a chart of the S&P 500. These highly variable astro events should be anticipated closely. Mark them on your calendar.

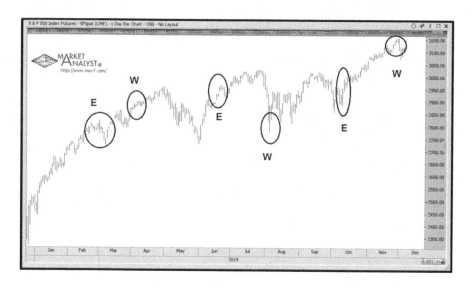

Figure 15
2019 Mercury Elongation events

For 2020, Mercury will be at greatest easterly elongation February 10, June 3 and October 1.

Greatest westerly elongation will occur March 24, July 22, and November 10.

Along the way, in addition to times of maximum elongation there will be retrograde events. Mercury retrograde is probably one of the most potent planetary influences for investors and traders to be aware of. We all too often hear about Mercury retrograde events in mundane Astrology. Do not sign important contracts during Mercury retrograde, do not cross the street, do not leave your house and so on. While I tend to ignore this mundane talk, I have noticed a striking correlation between financial market behavior and Mercury retrograde events.

To understand the science of Mercury retrograde, consider the diagram in Figure 16.

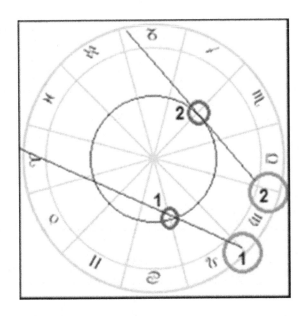

Figure 16
Mercury retrograde – The Concept

In 30 days of time planet Earth (shown as the larger circles in the diagram) will travel 30 degrees of the zodiac (from point 1 to point 2). But, Mercury is a faster mover. In the same 30 days of time, Mercury (shown as the smaller circles) will travel through about 120 degrees of the zodiac (point 1 to point 2) – passing by Earth in the process. From our vantage point here on Earth, initially as Mercury is setting up to pass Earth, we see Mercury in the sign of Aries. These sign determinations are made by extending a line from planet Earth through Mercury to the outer edge of the zodiac wheel. As Mercury completes its trip past Earth, we see it in the sign of Capricorn. In other words, the way we see it here on Earth, Mercury has moved backwards as it passed Earth. There is a curiously strong correlation between equity markets and Mercury retrograde events. Sometimes Mercury retrograde events encompass a sharp market inflection point. Sometimes a market peak or bottom will follow closely behind a retrograde event; sometimes a peak or bottom will immediately precede a retrograde event. When you know a Mercury retrograde event is approaching, use a suitable chart technical indicator such as DMI or Wilder Volatility Stop to determine if the price trend is changing.

Figure 17 illustrates some some 2018 and 2019 Mercury retrograde events overlaid on a chart of the S&P 500.

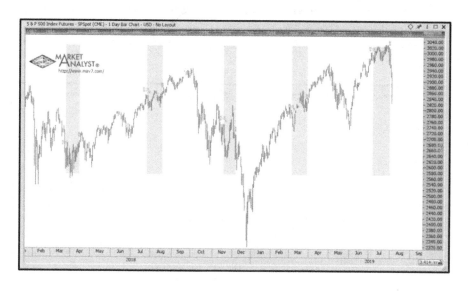

Figure 17
S&P 500 and Mercury retrograde

I think you will agree that Mercury retrograde events can be highly unpredictable. Sometimes in the course of a retrograde event a market index will decline and then recover all its losses. Other times, a Mercury retrograde event will trigger a trend change immediately prior or immediately after the onset of retrograde. When following

Mercury through its retrograde events, it is strongly advised to use shorter term charting and a good trend indicator tool.

Mercury retrograde events can often be seen influencing commodity markets too. Figure 18 illustrates the correlation between Copper futures prices and Mercury retrograde. While the average investor may not be aggressively trading Copper futures, this correlation could be used to better manage price risk of copper-related mining stocks in an investment portfolio. As I craft this manuscript, I note that in July 2019 Copper prices spiked briefly higher during a retrograde event, but then collapsed to make a low not seen since mid-2017.

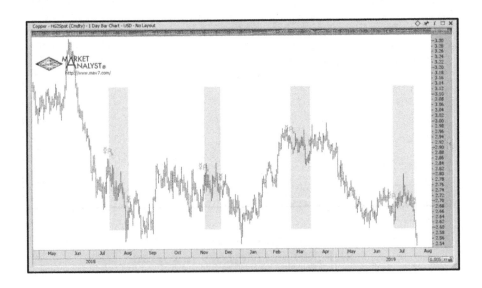

Figure 18
Mercury retrograde and Copper futures

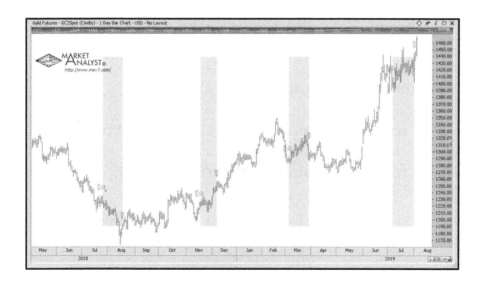

Figure 19
Mercury retrograde and Gold futures

Figure 19 illustrates Gold futures prices overlaid with Mercury retrograde events in 2018 and 2019. Note how Mercury retrograde events align to sharp price trend swings. Traders and investors who follow Gold futures or even Gold mining stocks may wish to rely on Mercury retrograde events when making buy and sell decisions. At the far right of Figure 19, a retrograde event can be seen. Immediately following this event, Gold prices climbed just over $110 per ounce. After preaking in September 2019, Gold prices gave up all this gain. At the retrograde event in November, prices stabilized and the trend started to turn positive again.

Whatever country you happen to reside in, check the major stock market index for that location to determine if there is a correlation to Mercury retrograde. If there is, take advantage of it. If trading commodity futures is not of interest to you, consider stocks related to commodities. In the case of Gold and Copper, take a look at gold and copper mining shares.

For 2020, Mercury will be:

> ➢ retrograde from February 17 through March 9.

> ➢ retrograde from June 18 through July 11.

> ➢ retrograde from October 14 through November 2.

CHAPTER SIX

Prof. Weston's Cycles

In 2017, late one night, whilst scouring the Internet looking for old Astrology manuscripts for sale, I came upon a white paper written in 1921 by a mysterious person going by the name of Professor Weston from Washington, D.C. I paid $50 for this product, and I am thrilled that I did. Never in my research travels to various libraries have I come across this name. I cannot find any other publications by him, although I understand there might be two more white papers out there somewhere. Who exactly he was, I will likely never know. Another one of those figures who emerged to write his ideas down and then vanished into the ether.

In his day, Weston analyzed copious amounts of data from the Dow Jones Average. He applied cosine Fourier mathematics and he came up with a general set of rules for the Dow. I have recently checked his model against the

Dow Jones over the past number of years and I find that his model is still accurate.

Perhaps Weston knew W.D. Gann. Perhaps he just knew of him. In any case, Weston followed the 20 year cycle of Jupiter and Saturn. He further broke this long cycle into two components of 10 years.

He went on to describe how investors can expect a 20 month cycle to begin in November of the 1st year of the 10 year cycle.

He said another 20 month cycle begins in November of the 5th year of the 10 year cycle.

He said 28 month cycles began in July of the 3rd and 7th years of the 10 year cycle.

A 10 month cycle begins in November of the 9th year of the 10 year cycle.

A 14 month cycle begins in September of the 10th year of the 10 year cycle.

The current Master Cycle started in June 2000. Following Weston's methodology, the first 20 month cycle would have started in November 2000 and went until July 2002.

A 28 month cycle then would have gone July 2002 through November 2004.

A 20 month cycle would then have followed until July 2006.

A 28 month cycle then ran July 2006 through November

2008.

A 10 month cycle then ran through until September 2009.

Lastly, a 14 month cycle lasted until November 2010.

For the second half of the Master Cycle, year 1 was 2010 (180 degree opposition of Saturn and Jupiter began late in 2010 and is exact very early in 2011), year 3 was 2012, year 5 was 2014, year 7 was 2016, year 9 was 2018 and year 10 was 2019. The next new Master Cycle will commence in November 2020.

For this new Master Cycle, the first 20 month Weston cycle will start in November 2020 and go until July 2022.

A 28 month cycle will go July 2022 through November 2024.

A 20 month cycle will then follow until July 2026.

A 28 month cycle will run July 2026 through November 2028.

A 10 month cycle will then go through until September 2029.

Lastly, a 14 month cycle will last until November 2030.

Weston also postulated that in the various years of a 10 year cycle, there would be market maxima as listed in Figure 20.

Year of Cycle	Maxima in	Maxima in
1	March	October
2		May
3	January	September
4	April	November
5	May	November
6		June
7	January	September
8		June
9	April	
10	February	August

Figure 20

Weston's Secondary Cycles

Weston also identified some secondary cycles within the 10 year half-Master cycles. He argued that the 16th Harmonic of a 10 year period (120 months) was actually the heliocentric periodicity of Venus. (120 x 30 / 16 = 225 days which is the time it takes Venus to orbit the Sun).

Looking closer at Weston's interval cycles, the 20 month cycle running from November 2010 through July 2012 is shown in Figure 21. The secondary maxima points have also been added to this chart in March and October 2011 and May 2012. I think we can all agree that these predicted maxima points were pretty good warning signs of market pullbacks.

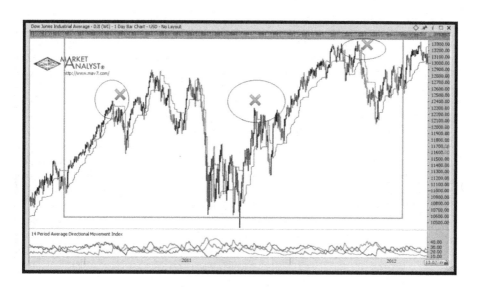

Figure 21
Weston's Secondary Maxima

The 28 month cycle running through to November 2014 is illustrated in Figure 22 with secondary maxima overlaid. There was a sharp pullback in late December 2012, which should have occurred in January 2013 according to Weston's secondary maxima model. The September 2013 maxima prediction aligned to an actual pullback. The April 2014 predicted maxima came with a 600 point pullback on the Dow. The November 2014 predicted maxima was if anything about a week early as the actual pullback occurred early in December.

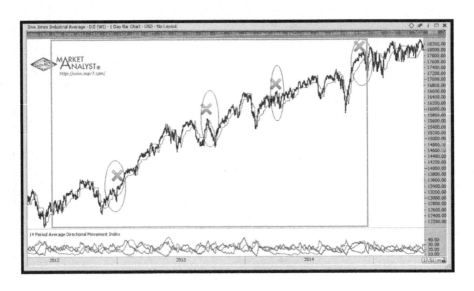

Figure 22
Weston's 28 Month Cycle

What follows next is a 20 month cycle as illustrated in Figure 23 which runs November 2014 through July 2016. The secondary maxima points have also been added for May and November 2015 and June 2016. These predicted points all seem to align to some downwards price action. A maxima point has been added for January 2017. Not more than 150 points of pullback occurred at this predicted event, but a maxima did shave nearly 80 points off the S&P 500 starting late February just ahead of a Venus retrograde event.

The 28 month cycle, which Weston says ran from July 2016 to November 2018, was punctuated by the Congressional mid-term elections in America. Was it the election outcome that influenced the market or was it merely cyclical astrological behavior?

September 2017, according to Weston, should have seen a

secondary maxima (it actually came in August), as should have June 2018 (S&P 500 lost nearly 100 points in June, 2018). April 2019 was to have seen a maxima event. In fact, it came starting on May 1 and the S&P 500 lost just shy of 200 points. February and August 2020 should see maxima as well.

A 10 month cycle will then take us to September 2019 and a 14 month cycle will take us to November 2020 and the start of a new Master Cycle.

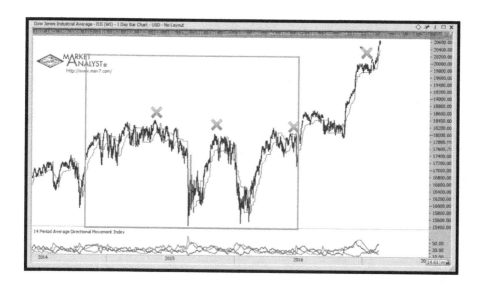

Figure 23
Weston's 20 Month Cycle

CHAPTER SEVEN

Sacred Cycles

Cyclical occurrences from the world of religion have a curious way of intersecting with financial market turning points. One religious conceot is that of *Shmitah* which is rooted in the Hebrew Bible.

In the book of Exodus (Chapter 23, verses 10-11), it is written:

"You may plant your land for six years and gather its crops. But during the seventh year, you must leave it alone and withdraw from it."

In the book of Leviticus (Chapter 25, verses 20-22), it is written:

"And if ye shall say: 'What shall we eat the seventh year? behold, we may not sow, nor gather in our increase'; then I will

command My blessing upon you in the sixth year, and it shall bring forth produce for the three years. And ye shall sow the eighth year, and eat of the produce, the old store; until the ninth year, until her produce come in, ye shall eat the old store."

I first learned of the Shmitah when I was introduced several years ago to the writings of Rabbi Jonathan Cahn. He has done a masterful job of applying Shmitah to the paradigm of the financial markets.

Breaking these Biblical statements down into simple to understand terms means that every 7th year something will happen on the financial markets.

The first Shmitah year in the modern State of Israel was 1951-52 (5712 in the Hebrew calendar). Subsequent Shmita years have been 1958–59 (5719), 1965–66 (5726), 1972–73 (5733), 1979–80 (5740), 1986–87 (5747), 1993–94 (5754), 2000–01 (5761), 2007–08 (5768), and 2014-15 (5775). The next Shmita year will be 2021-2022 (5782). A Shemitah Year starts in the month of Tishrei (the first month of the Jewish civil Calendar) and ends in the month of Elul.

The chart in Figure 24 illustrates the S&P 500 with some recent Shmitah years overlaid. I trust you can see how the select few who understand Shmitah would have profited handsomely from these moves on the S&P 500.

Figure 24
S&P 500 and Shmitah years

Shmitah years are not always about the equity markets. The chart in Figure 25 illustrates Oil prices with Shmitah years overlaid. Again, the select few who understand Shmitah made serious money on the Crude Oil market.

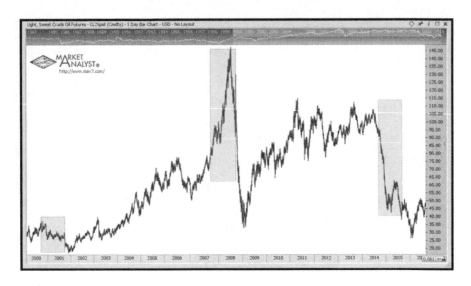

Figure 25
Crude Oil and Shmitah years

Let's now circle back to the above Biblical passages. The message is, there shall be no crop in the Shmitah year. In the year after the Shmitah, people shall live on the bounty of the crop produced in year 6 – the year immediately prior to Shmitah. In the 9th year, the newly planted crop will come in.

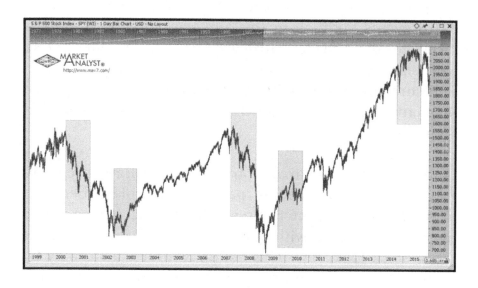

Figure 26
The Aftermath of Shmitah years

In Figure 26, which illustrates price action on the S&P 500, I have left a gap to represent the year following Shmitah. I have then placed another rectangle to mark what effectively is the second year after Shmitah. Note what happens in the year immediately after Shmitah – the market actually falls and takes out the lows of the Smhitah year. But not to worry – because the Bible says we are to be living off the produce harvested (financial gains made) prior to Shmitah. Look what happens next. The market gets back its footing and starts to climb.

What are the implications for traders and investors here and now? The Shmitah year ended in September 2015. We wrapped up the post Shmitah year in September 2016. Starting in the Fall of 2016, the markets regained their footing (on the heels of a Donald Trump electoral win) and started to inch higher. True, there has been volatility and uncertainty both and lots of it – driven by the various astro events outlined in this almanac. But the trend has been to the upside. However, do not be lulled into complacency. If you decide to follow the Shmitah measure of time, take your profits in the period September 2020-2021. Plan to re-enter the markets in September 2023.

Religious cycles as a market trading tool still require more back-testing work on my part. In particular, there are certain dates from the Hebrew calendar that have a strong propensity to align with swing highs and lows on the New York Stock Exchange. This notion is hinted at strongly by Rabbi Jonathan Cahn in his writings pertaining to the 7 year Shmitah cycle. Rabbi Cahn says to pay close attention to four dates from the Hebrew calendar.

In particular, the 1st Day of the month of Tishrei marks the start of the Jewish civil calendar, much like January 1 marks the start of the Gregorian calendar that I follow.

The 1st day of the month of Nissan marks the start of the Jewish sacred year.

The 3rd important date is the 9th Day of the month of Av which marks the date when Babylon destroyed the Temple at Jerusalem in 586 BC. Other calamitous events have beset the Jewish people on the 9th of Av throughout history. In particular, Cahn tells of the mass expulsion of Jewish people from Spain in 1492. As this expulsion was going on, a certain explorer with 3 ships was about to set sail on a voyage of discovery. That explorer sailed out of port on August 3, 1492 which was one day after the 9th of Av. That explorer – indeed was Christopher Columbus and he found the New World and as Cahn tells it – that New World became a new home for the Jewish people.

The 4th key date in the Jewish calendar is Shemini Atzeret (The Gathering of the Eighth Day). This date typically falls somewhere in late September through late October in the month of Tishrei. I found a helpful website at *www.chabad.org* that allows me to quickly scan back over a number of years to pick off these important dates. I have examined price action on the Dow Jones Average across several years in the context of these key dates. My backtesting has shown a variable correlation to these dates. But, the correlation is intriguing enough that I now recommend that traders and investors pay attention to thse dates.

For 2019, these key Hebrew calendar dates fell as follows:

1st of Nissan was April 6, the 9th of Av was August 10, the 1st of Tishrei was September 30 and Shemini Atzeret was October 21.

For 2020, these dates will be: 1st of Nissan on March 26, the 9th of Av on July 30, the 1st of Tishrei on September 19 and Shemini Atzeret on October 10.

I recently happened upon a 2005 past edition of *Trader's World* magazine, and in it an article referring to W.D. Gann. The article suggested he might have been instilled with knowledge of Jewish mysticism – more commonly known as the Kabbalah. Gann apparently had connections to a New York personality called Sepharial who is said to have taught Gann about astrology and esoteric matters.

The Kabbalah centers around the Hebrew Alef-bet (we would call it an alphabet in English). The Hebrew Alef-bet comprises 22 letters. In Kabbalistic methodology, these letters are assigned a numerical value. Starting with the first letter, values are 1,2,3,4,5,6,7,8,9,10, 20,30,40,50,60,70,80,90,100,200,300,400.

There are many mathematical techniques that can be applied to parsing the Alef-bet. One in particular involves taking the odd-numbered letters and the even numbered letters and assigning their appropriate numerical values.

The numerical value (sum total) of the Alef-bet is 1495.

The sum total of the odd-numbered letters is 625. The sum total of the even numbered letters is 870.

625 / 1495 = 42%. Taking a circle of 360 degrees, 42% is 150.5 degrees.

870 / 1495 = 58%. Taking a circle of 360 degrees, 58% is 209.5 degrees.

Kabbalists are also well aware of *phi* as it pertains to the Golden Mean. Phi is famously known as 1.618.

1/phi = 62%. Taking a circle of 360 degrees, 62% is 222.5 degrees.

1 – (1/phi) = 48%. Taking a circle of 360 degrees, 48% is 137.5 degrees.

From a significant price low (or high), one might wish to look for time intervals when a geocentric or heliocentric planet advances these degree amounts.

To illustrate, consider the significant low in March 2009 on US equity markets (S&P 500) as a start point. Over ten years later, Figure 27 shows that 150.5 degree advancements of heliocentric Venus come perilously close to aligning with significant swings on the S&P 500.

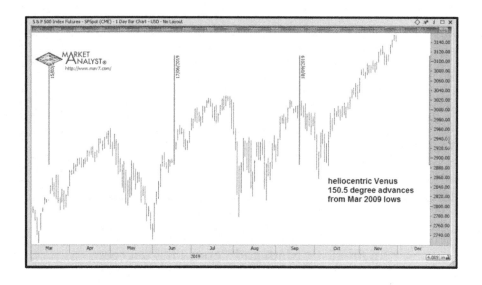

Figure 27
Kabbalistic Math and Venus 150.5 degrees

Using the phi approach, Figure 28 shows that from the March 2009 lows, over ten years later, 137.5 degree advancements of heliocentric Venus come perilously close to aligning with significant swings on the S&P 500. When I say perilously close, I am talking up to two weeks close. Over a span of 10 years (520 weeks), I regard this as significant.

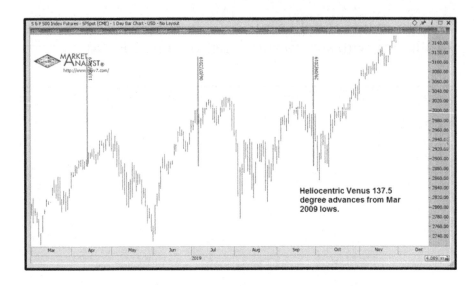

Figure 28

Kabbalistic Math and Venus 137.5 degrees

To further illustrate, consider the 2011 significant high for Gold. Over eight years later, Figure 29 shows how the 150.5 degree advancements of heliocentric Venus come perilously close to aligning with significant swings on Gold price.

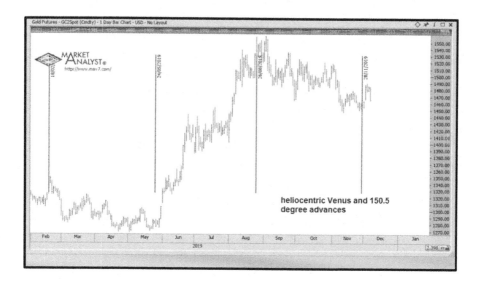

Figure 29
Kabbalistic Math and Gold

CHAPTER EIGHT

Cyclical Intervals

Astrologers measure time by *synodic cycles* and *sidereal cycles*. A sidereal cycle is one that is measured from the vantage point of the Sun. If an observer were standing on the Sun, he or she would see Venus travel around the Sun one complete time in 225 days. Mars would take 687 days. The outer planets would take much longer. In fact, Saturn would take 29.42 years, Uranus 83.75 years, Neptune 163.74 years and Pluto 245.33 years.

A synodic cycle is measured from the vantage point of here on Earth. To an observer standing here on terra firma, the time it takes Venus to record a conjunction with Sun until that same conjunction occurs again appears to be 584 days. Mars takes 780 days from Sun/Mars conjunction to the next Sun/Mars conjunction. Saturn takes 376 days and the other outer planets 367 to 399 days.

The sidereal cycles of the outer planets seem to bear an

alignment to larger events in history. For example, the year 1776 is key to American history. Add a Neptune cycle to 1776 and one gets 1939 — when the world was on the cusp of World War 2. The American Civil War started in 1861 with the events at Fort Sumter. Add a Uranus cycle to this date and one gets to the time when World War 2 ended. Add another Uranus cycle and that takes us to 2028. Are we headed for another major conflict? Current events in the world would lead one to think so.

The Moon has synodic and sidereal cycles as well. The sidereal period of the Moon is 27.5 days and the synodic period is 29.53 days. This latter period is where we get the expression *lunar month*. During each sidereal lunar cycle, the Moon can be seen to vary in its position above and below the lunar ecliptic. In other words, in a sidereal period, the Moon will go from maximum declination to maximum declination. It is said that W.D. Gann was a proponent of following lunar cycles when trading Soybeans and Cotton. And, why not? After all, the Moon's gravitational pull governs the ocean tides. Our bodies are substantially water, so it stands to reason that the Moon will influence our behaviors which in turn will affect the markets. Take a look at a daily chart of a stock you like to trade or invest in. Take a look at a commodity futures contract you follow. You will often find that at times of maximum or minimum lunar declination there will be a short term change in price behavior best witnessed on an hourly chart setup. Figure 30 presents a chart of Soybeans with the Moon declination in the lower panel. Note the propensity for declination maxima to align to trend changes. A 4 hour chart would be the ideal way to study these price swings closely. You can see why a trader like W.D. Gann would have used this declination phenomenon to give himself an advantage in the markets.

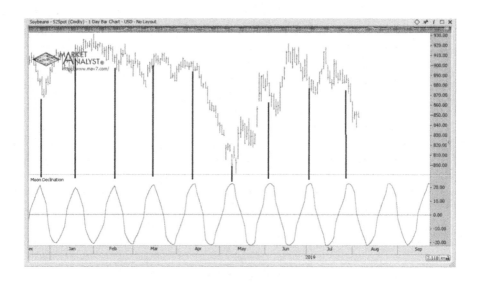

Figure 30
Moon Declination and Soybeans

Figure 31 illustrates Cotton futures prices during 2019 to date. I have overlaid the chart with a dark vertical line at the maximum lunar declination events and also the minimum declination events that also align to trend changes. Again, you can get a sense for why someone like W.D. Gann might have used declination when trading Cotton futures.

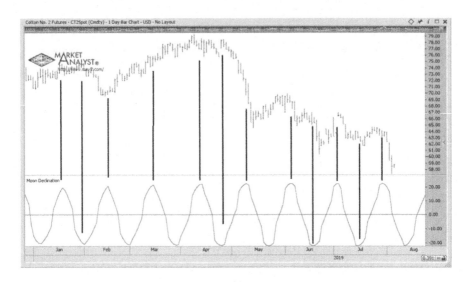

Figure 31
Moon Declination and Cotton

To assist you in some back-testing of your own, consider that in 2018, Moon recorded maximums in its declination on January 2, January 29, February 26, March 25, April 22, May 19, June 15, July 12, August 9, September 5, October 2, October 30, November 26 and December 23.

In 2018, Moon recorded minimums in its declination on January 16, February 12, March 11, April 7, May 5, June 1, June 28, July 26, August 22, September 18, October 16, November 12 and December 9.

For 2019, Moon recorded maximums in its declination on January 20, February 16, March 15, April 12, May 9, June 5, July 2, July 30, August 26, September 23, October 19, November 17 and December 14.

2019 lunar declination minima occurred on February 2, March 1, March 28, April 26, May 22, June 19, July 17, August 13, September 8, October 5, November 2,

November 30, and December 27.

For 2020, Moon will record declination maxima on January 10, February 6, March 5, April 1, April 29, May 25, June 22, July 19, August 16, September 12, October 9, November 5, December 4, December 30. Declination minima will occur January 23, February 19, March 18, April 14, May 11, June 7, July 5, August 1, August 29, September 25, October 22, November 18, and December 16.

There are also cyclical intervals that relate to Pythagorean mathematics. Imagine if you will a square with each side being 1000 units long. Now imagine a circle that is inscribed into that square. The diameter of that circle will of course be 1000 units.

Next, recall from your mathematics classes the peculiar feature of 'pi' which carries the value 1.34159.

The circumference of the circle inscribed into the square will be pi x diameter. In this case pi x 1000 = 3141.159 units.

The perimeter of the square will be the sum total of the four sides, 1000 + 1000 + 1000 +1000 = 4000.

The ratio of the perimeter to the circumference of the circle is 4000 / 3141.159 = 1.2734. This figure times 1000 equals 1273.4.

Next, imagine the square cut diagonally across. If the sides of the square are each 1000 units, the length of the diagonal is defined by the Pythagorean equation $a^2 + b^2 = c^2$. The diagonal is thus defined by $(1000)^2 + (1000)^2 = c^2 = 1414.21$ units. The ratio of the diagonal to the perimeter of the square is 1414.21/4000 = 0.3536.

Next imagine a square with sides equal to 1273. The diagonal calculates as $(1273)^2 + (1273)^2 = c^2 = 1800.3$ units.

Consider now multiplying 0.3536 by 1800.3 and one gets 636.6.

Next imagine a right angled triangle with one side being 1 unit long and another side being 2 units long. The Pythagorean expression $(1)^2 + (2)^2 = c^2$ can be used to define the length of the longest side (the hypoteneuse). In this case, c = 2.2361 units. Now, add the length of all three sides and divide by the length of the longest side (the hypoteneuse). This works out to (1 + 2 + 2.2361) / 2.2361 = 2.3416 units.

Consider next the sum of the two sides divided by the hypoteneuse. This works out to (2 + 1)/2.2361 = 1.3416.

Next, recall from your mathematics classes that a circle contains 360 degrees. Another unit of measure for expressing this is *radians* where 360 degrees equals 2 x pi radians. In our right angled triangle with sides of 1,2 and 2.2361 units, the angles in that triangle will necessarily be 30, 60 and 90 degrees. An angle of 60 degrees equals pi / 3 radians.

Consider now a circle of diameter 1000 units inscribed in a square with sides of 1000 units. The expression (pi x 1000) / 3 = 1047.2 units.

Double this figure and one gets 2094.4 units.

Consider now a right angled triangle with sides of 1047.2

and 2094.4. The Pythagorean theorem for determining the length of the hypoteneuse is $(1047.2)^2 + (2094.4)^2 = c^2$. Solving for c yields 2341.6.

So, taking all of the above calculated numbers in these various complicated mathematical expressions and rounding them off slightly gives us the following sequence of numbers: 637, 1047, 1273, 1341, 1414, 1800, 2094, 2341, and 4242.

From a significant low (or high) on a commodity, a stock or an index, plot these calendar intervals on the chart and you will notice a very high propensity for the intervals to align to points of trend change.

To illustrate, consider the price chart of Gold in Figure 32 where I have selected the 1999 price low as a start point. Note how the various intervals align to inflection points on the chart.

If you are wondering where this bit of complex math comes from, credit goes to Bill Erman who passed away in 2016. He called his mathematical approach *Ermanometry*. Let us not forget his good work.

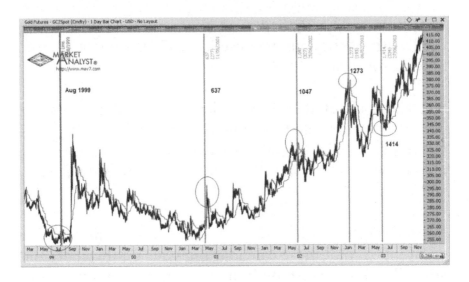

Figure 32
Gold and Ermanometry Intervals

Let's now consider another example. Take the 2012 extreme high recorded on Soybeans. Figure 33 presents the first of the Ermanometry intervals. Note the curious alignment to points of trend change. Figure 34 brings the Soybean chart up to the present time. January 2019 marked a 2341 day interval after which prices sold off.

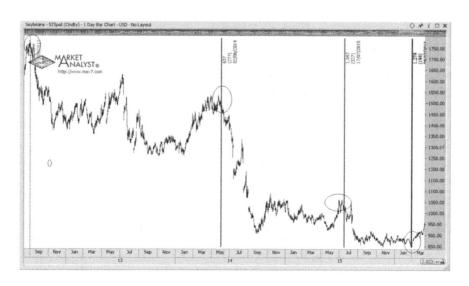

Figure 33
Soybeans and Ermanometry Intervals

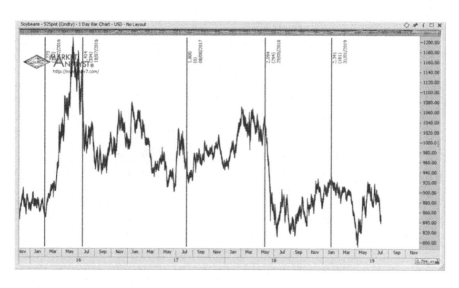

Figure 34
Soybeans and additional Ermanometry Intervals

Turning to the S&P 500, if I apply these intervals starting at a low point in early February 2016, the plot in Figure 35 illustrates how well the alignment is. The August 2019 peak that led to a violent sell-off with China being labelled a currency manipulator aligns perfectly to an Ermanometry 1273 day interval.

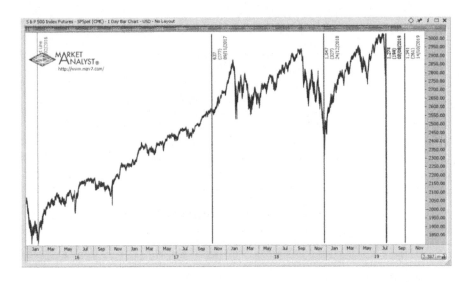

Figure 35
S&P 500 and additional Ermanometry Intervals

So, look at a chart of interest to you, identify a significant high or low turning point and then apply the calendar day intervals 637, 1047, 1273, 1341, 1414, 1800, 2094, 2341, and 4242 days and you now have a powerful market timing tool at your fingertips.

CHAPTER NINE

Parallel and Contra Parallel

As the various celestial bodies make their respective journeys around the Sun, they can be seen to move relative to our vantage point of the celestial equator. Declination refers to the positioning of a celestial body above or below the celestial equator plane. Celestial bodies experience declinations of up to about 25 degrees above and below the celestial equator plane.

Declination can be viewed one planet at a time or by pairs of planets. Let's suppose that at a particular time Mars can be seen as being 10 degrees of declination above the celestial equator and at that same time Venus is also at 10 degrees of declination. Let's further suppose that we allow for up to 1.5 degrees tolerance in our measurement of declinations. We would say these two planets were at *parallel declination*. Let's take another example and suppose that at a given time Jupiter was at 5 degrees of declination above the celestial equator and at that same time period

Pluto was at 6.5 degrees declination below the celestial equator. Again, let's allow for up to 1.5 degrees of tolerance. We would say that Jupiter and Pluto were at *contra-parallel declination*. Parallel and contra-parallel events have a powerful bearing on certain aspects of the financial markets.

I have spent many hours exploring parallel and contra-parallel events with respect to commodity futures contracts. This research was spurred on by a 25 year old Astrology book I found in a used bookshop in early 2017. In studying this old book, I have found there are some commodities that in fact bear a correlation to the same parallel and contra-parallel conditions that were in place at the First Trade date. I strongly suggest using these parallel and contra-parallel events in combination with the other astrology events outlined throughout this almanac. Using a suitable software program or reliable on-line source, obtain the planetary declinations at the first trade date for the stock or commodity in question. Examine the data for evidence of parallel and contra parallel events. Watch for these parallel and contra-parallel occurrences to repeat themselves at future dates. These dates may align to short term trend changes. To illustrate, the following Gold, Cotton, Crude Oil, and Soybeans studies show you how it is done. This is still very much a work in progress for me and much remains to be studied yet.

Gold

Gold futures started trading in New York on Dec 31, 1974. At that date, the planets were at the following declinations relative to the ecliptic:

Sun	-23.06 degrees
Venus	-22.42 degrees
Mars	-22.45 degrees
Jupiter	-7.39 degrees
Saturn	+22.05 degrees
Uranus	-11.37 degrees
Neptune	-20.3 degrees
Pluto	+11.44 degrees

Looking closer at these numbers we can see the following:

Uranus is contra-parallel to Pluto (contra-parallel = declinations within 1.5 degrees of each other, but signs are opposite)

Saturn is contra-parallel Mars

Saturn is contra-parallel Venus

Saturn is contra-parallel Sun

Mars is parallel Sun (parallel = declinations with 1.5 degrees of each other, signs are the same)

Mars is parallel Venus

Sun is parallel Venus

For 2019, Mars was parallel Sun from June 4 to 24 and again August 13 to September 6.

For 2019, Mars was parallel Venus from June 17 to July 4 and August 15 to September 2.

For 2019, Sun was parallel Venus June 22 to July 15, August

15 to September 2, December 10 to 20.

For 2019, Saturn was contra-parallel Sun from May 24 through July 18.

For 2019, Saturn was contra-parallel Venus from June 14 to July 30.

The price chart of Gold in Figure 36 has been overlaid with some of these events from 2019. Gold staged a powerful rally from late May 2019 in response to global trade disputes. I find it curiously interesting how the onset of this rally aligned to some of these astro events.

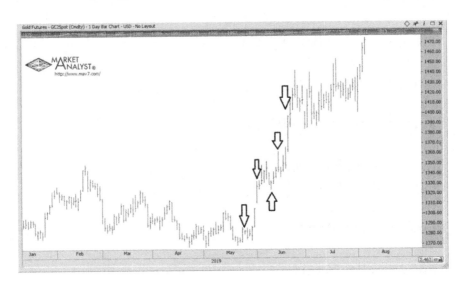

Figure 36
Gold and Declination Phenomenon

For 2020, Mars will parallel Sun for 4 days either side of January 14 and again September 5.

Mars will parallel Venus for about 6 days either side of October 15.

Sun will parallel Venus for about 4 days either side of June 4.

Saturn will be contra-parallel Venus March 24 through 31.

Saturn will be contra-parallel Sun from May 26 through June 10.

Cotton

Cotton futures started trading in New York on June 20, 1870. At that date, the planets were at the following declinations relative to the ecliptic:

Sun	+23.45 degrees
Venus	+14.84 degrees
Mars	+21.42 degrees
Jupiter	+21.32 degrees
Saturn	-22.09 degrees
Uranus	+22.31 degrees
Neptune	+6.86 degrees
Pluto	+2.99 degrees

Looking closer at these numbers we can see the following:

Sun is contra-parallel to Saturn

Sun is parallel Uranus

Saturn is contra-parallel Uranus

Uranus is parallel Jupiter

Uranus is parallel Mars

Mars is parallel Jupiter

Mars is contra-parallel Saturn

Mars is parallel Uranus

For 2019, Saturn was contra-parallel Sun from May 28 through July 19.

For 2019 Sun was parallel Uranus from April 14 to April 25.

2019 saw Uranus parallel Mars from February 4 to 17 and August 7 to 23.

In 2019, Mars was contra parallel Saturn from April 7 through July 5.

The price chart of Cotton in Figure 37 has been overlaid with some of these events from 2019. The alignment to trend change points is more than just a little curious.

For 2020, Saturn will be contra-parallel May 26 through June 10.

Sun will parallel Uranus for about 6 days either side of April 25.

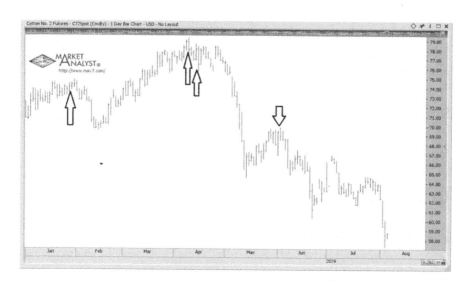

Figure 37
Cotton and Declination Phenomenon

Crude Oil

Crude Oil futures started trading in America on March 30, 1983. At that date, the planets were at the following declinations relative to the ecliptic:

Sun	+3.52 degrees
Venus	+16.28 degrees
Mercury	+4.38
Mars	+9.52 degrees
Jupiter	-21.18 degrees
Saturn	-9.87 degrees
Uranus	-21.70 degrees
Neptune	-22.20 degrees
Pluto	+5.42 degrees

Looking closer at these numbers we can see the following:

Sun is parallel to Pluto (declinations within 2 degrees of each other, signs are the same)

Sun is parallel Mercury

Mars is contra-parallel Saturn

Uranus is parallel Jupiter

Uranus is parallel Neptune

Jupiter is parallel Neptune

For 2019, Sun was parallel Pluto from January 1 to January 23 and again from Nov 27 to year end.

There was one Mars contra-parallel Saturn events in 2019 from April 1 through July 4.

There were numerous Sun parallel Mercury events in 2019 including February 3 to 9, March 15 to 21, May 17 to 23, June 14 to 20, July 31 to August 5, September 5 to 11, November 8 to 14, and December 20 to 24.

The price chart of Crude Oil in Figure 38 has been overlaid with some of these events from 2019. Note how so many price swings and inflections coincide with these declination events, especially the Mercury events.

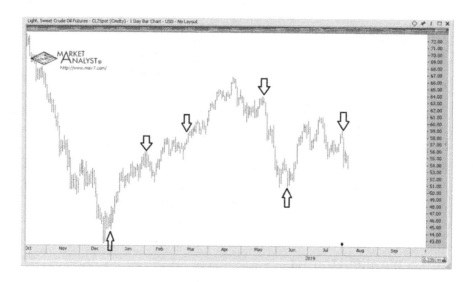

Figure 38
Crude Oil and Declination Phenomenon

For 2020, Sun will parallel Pluto from January 1 through 21.

Sun will parallel Mercury for about 3 days either side of January 21, March 1, May 4, June 11, July 21, August 21, October 26, and December 12.

Soybeans

As will be discussed in a coming chapter, the Chicago Board of Trade was founded April 3, 1848. Looking at Soybean futures through the lens of this date as opposed to the 1936 date when Soybean futures actually started trading yields some interesting finds. At the 1848 date, the planets were at the following declinations relative to the ecliptic:

Sun	+5.35 degrees
Venus	-7.26 degrees
Mercury	-6.10
Mars	+24.80 degrees
Jupiter	+23.26 degrees
Saturn	-6.08 degrees
Uranus	+6.48 degrees
Neptune	-11.48 degrees
Pluto	-5.46 degrees

Sun is parallel Uranus

Sun is contra parallel Pluto, Venus, Mercury and Saturn

Mercury is parallel Saturn

Mercury is contra parallel Uranus

Mars is parallel Jupiter

In 2019, Sun was parallel Uranus April 14 to 25.

In 2019, Sun was contra parallel Saturn from May 28 to July 19.

Sun was contra-parallel Pluto May 20 to June 11 and again June 29 through July 21st.

The price chart of Soybeans in Figure 39 has been overlaid with some of these events from 2019.

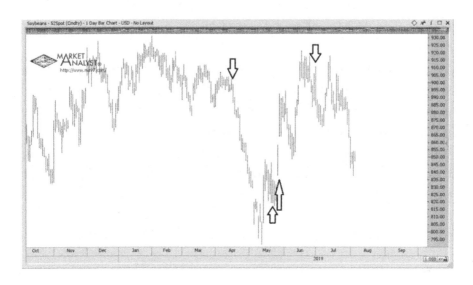

Figure 39
Soybeans (1848) and Declination Phenomenon

For 2020, Sun will be parallel Uranus from April 21 to 27.

Sun will be contra parallel Saturn frm May 14 through June 4.

Sun will be contra parallel Pluto from May 18 through June 17.

Mars will be parallel Jupiter from March 10 through April 15.

As for the New York Stock Exchange, an examination of planetary positions at May 17, 1792 reveals Mercury and Uranus were parallel and Jupiter was parallel to Neptune. In 2019, the sell-off that started in early May aligned to a Mercury-Uranus parallel.

For 2020, Mercury will parallel Uranus for about 5 days

either side of May 2 and August 18.

With the aid of either a table of declination data or a suitable internet website, you can obtain the declinations at a first trade date for stocks of your choosing. Take the parallel and contra-parallel findings from that first trade date and mark similar occurences on your trading calendar for 2020. You now have another powerful tool at your disposal.

CHAPTER TEN

NYSE 2020 Astrology

The brief introduction to Louise McWhirter in an earlier chapter opens the door to a look at the astrology of the New York Stock Exchange. During her lifetime, Louise McWhirter focused intently on the astrology of the New York Exchange. Her technique which revolves around the New Moon (lunation) remains viable to this day.

The Lunation and the New York Stock Exchange

A *lunation* is the astrological term for a New Moon. At a lunation, the Sun and Moon are separated by 0 degrees which means the Sun and Moon are together in the same sign of the zodiac. The correlation between the monthly lunation event and New York Stock Exchange price movements was first popularized in 1937 by McWhirter. In her book, *Theory of Stock Market Forecasting*, she discussed how a lunation making hard aspects to planets such as Mars, Jupiter, Saturn and Uranus was indicative of a coming month of volatility on the New York Stock Exchange. She also paid close attention to Mars and Neptune - the two planets that *rule* the New York Stock Exchange. McWhirter said those times of a lunar month when the transiting Moon makes 0 degree aspects to Mars and Neptune should be watched carefully. The concept of *planetary rulership* extends back into the 1800s with each zodiac sign having a planet that rules that sign. McWhirter arrived at her Mars and Neptune rulership conclusion by observing that the 10th House of the 1792 birth horoscope wheel for the NYSE spans Pisces and Aries. Neptune rules Pisces and Mars rules Aries.

New York Stock Exchange – First Trade Chart

The New York Stock Exchange officially opened for business on May 17, 1792. As the horoscope in Figure 40 shows, the NYSE has its Ascendant (Asc) at 14 degrees Cancer and its Mid-Heaven (MC) at 24 Pisces.

McWhirter further paid close attention to those times in the monthly lunar cycle when the transiting Moon passed by the NYSE natal Asc and MC locations at 14 Cancer and 24 Pisces respectively.

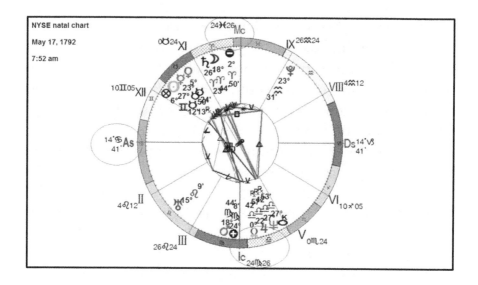

Figure 40
NYSE First Trade horoscope

Horoscope Charts and the McWhirter Methodology

In my research and writing, I follow the McWhirter methodology. When forecasting whether or not a coming month will be volatile or not for the NYSE, the McWhirter methodology starts with creating a horoscope chart for the New Moon date and positioning the Ascendant of the chart at 14 degrees Cancer. This point in the sign of Cancer is the Ascendant position on the 1792 natal chart of the New York Stock Exchange. Positioning the Ascendant is made easy in the Solar Fire Gold software program. Aspects to the lunation are then studied. If the lunation is at a 0, 90 or 120 degree aspect to Mars, Neptune, 14 Cancer or 24 Pisces, one can expect a volatile month ahead. A lack of such aspects portends a less volatile period. Using Solar Fire Gold software I then advance the horoscope forward one day at a time watching where Moon is at each day.

Aspects of the Moon to Mars, Neptune, 14 Cancer or 24 Pisces represent dates of potential trend reversals. I further pay attention to those dates when Moon is at either maximum or minimum declination. I keep in mind those dates when Mercury is retrograde and those dates when Venus is at or near its maximum or minimum declination. When I see multiple overlapping events I pay extremely close attention.

Similarly, when studying an individual stock or an individual commodity futures contract, the McWhirter approach calls for the creation of a horoscope chart at the First Trade date of the stock or commodity. The Ascendant is then shifted so that the Sun is at the Ascendant. Again, the software program Solar Fire Gold is very good for generating First Trade horoscope charts for McWhirter analysis where the Ascendant needs to be shifted. Why she insists on having Sun at the Ascendant, I do not know. I simply follow her routine.

In stock and commodity analyses, McWhirter then paid strict attention to those times of a calendar year when transiting Sun, Mars, Jupiter, Saturn, Neptune and Uranus made hard 0, 90 and 180 degree aspects to the natal Mid-Heaven, natal Ascendant, natal Sun, natal Jupiter and even the natal Moon of the individual stock or commodity future being studied.

One must be alert at these aspects for the possibility of a trend change, the possibility of increased volatility within a trend or even the possibility of a breakout from a chart consolidation pattern. Evidence of such trend changes will be found by watching price action relative to moving averages and by utilizing oscillator type functions (MAC-D, DMI, RSI and so on). This almanac assumes that the reader is reasonably well versed in chart technical analysis.

McWhirter Lunation Past Example

To set the stage for the remainder of this chapter, the following example of the McWhirter method is taken from the 2018 version of the Financial Astrology Almanac. My synopsis, written many months in advance of this actual event, stated:

The New Moon occurs on the 6th of December with Sun at 14 degrees Sagittarius. This lunation is a powerful one. Co-rulers Mars and Neptune are conjunct and the lunation is a hard 90 degree square to this conjunct pair. This lunar cycle runs through to January 6, 2019 so expect some volatile action. With Mercury just having finished its retrograde event, I would not be shocked to see a positive market reaction during this cycle.

I further pointed out that on December 23rd, transiting Moon would pass the NYSE natal Ascendant point at 14 Cancer.

As the S&P 500 chart in Figure 41 shows, there was a frightening drawdown on the equity market and fear was setting in before Treasury Secretary Steven Mnuchin issued calming sentiment. But, maybe his words were not even necessary for just as he spoke, Moon was passing 14 Cancer which has a stunning correlation to trend reversals on the S&P 500 and Dow Jones Average.

Figure 41
Lunation event Late 2018

Let's now examine the lunation events for 2020.

2020 Lunation Forecasts

December 2019 – January 2020

The New Moon cycle starting December 26th with Sun at 3 Capricorn will set the stage for the start of the 2020 trading year. The horoscope in Figure 42 depicts planetary placements hours before the New Moon event as the Ascendant passes 14 Cancer.

There are no unfavorable aspects to this lunation. The one feature of note is the lunation is conjunct to Jupiter. Such conunctions have the potential to align to a change of trend on the S&P 500. The change of trend need not be dramatic.

Key dates to be alert to during this lunar cycle include:

December 31: Moon passes NYSE co-ruler Nepture. This date will likely be a light trading day so this transit should be tame.

January 1: Market will be closed as Moon transits the natal mid-Heaven point of 24 Pisces.

January 7-8: Moon passes 90 degrees to Neptune.

January 9: Moon will pass the NYSE natal Ascendant point of 14 Cancer.

January 10: Moon at maximum declination. This January 9-10th, 2 day combination of events will likely cause some added volatility to appear on equity markets. In addition, the period January 9th through 17th will see Sun transit past

Saturn. This conjunction event has a *strong* propensity to align to trend changes on equity markets.

January 13: Moon passes 90 degrees to Mars.

January 20: Moon passes NYSE co-ruler Mars.

January 23: Moon at minimum declination. European Central Bank (ECB) meets to discuss monetary policy.

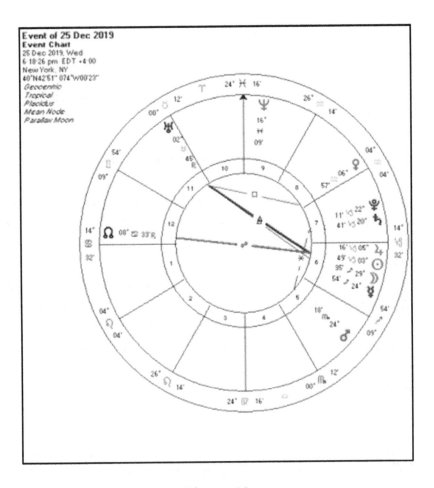

Figure 42
New Moon December 26, 2019

January - February 2020

Market action from late January through late February will be influenced by the New Moon cycle that commences on January 24 with Sun at 3 Aquarius. This lunar cycle runs until February 23. The horoscope in Figure 43 depicts planetary placements hours before the New Moon event as the Ascendant passes 14 Cancer.

Co-rulers Mars and Neptune are at a 90 degree aspect to each other and the lunation itself rests mid-way between these two rulers. This unique placement should stir up some energy across the equity market spectrum. As well, co-ruler Neptune is within orb of being at the natal mid-heaven point which should add to the energy.

Key dates to be alert to during this lunar cycle include:

January 28-29: Moon is conjunct co-ruler Neptune and 90 degrees to co-ruler Mars at the same time. This should add to market *volatility*. Moon also transits past the 24 Pisces natal mid-Heaven point. The FOMC meets to discuss monetary policy.

February 4-6: Moon passes 90 degrees to Neptune and also is at maximum declination. In addition, Moon passes the 14 of Cancer point. This three day time span should see added market volatility.

February 11: Moon passes 90 degrees to Mars.

February 17: Mercury turns retrograde and remains so until March 9.

February 18-19: Moon at minimum declination while it

transits past Mars.

February 20: Mars is at its minimu declination, but the approach to thisminimum started late January and will go to mid-March.

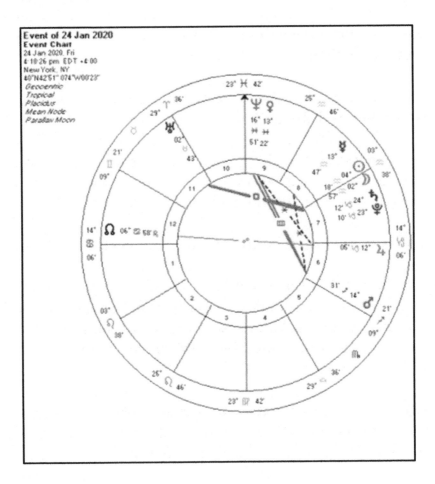

Figure 43
New Moon January 24, 2020

February - March 2020

Market action from late February through late March will be influenced by the New Moon cycle that commences on February 23 with Sun at 4 Pisces. The horoscope in Figure 44 depicts planetary placements hours before the New Moon event as the Ascendant passes 14 Cancer.

This lunation makes a favorable 60 degree aspect to co-ruler Mars. There are no other untoward aspects visible in the horoscope. However, during this lunation Mercury will turn retrograde. Retrograde events have a serious track record for aligning to sudden, sharp price action on equity markets.

Key dates to be alert to in this lunation include:

February 24-25: Moon transits past co-ruler Neptune as well as the natal mid-Heaven point of 24 Pisces.

February 26: Moon passes 90 degrees square to co-ruler Mars.

March 2-3: Moon passes 90 degrees square to co-ruler Neptune.

March 5: Moon passes the 14 of Cancer point and records its maximum declination at the same time. This should impart added energy and volatility to the equity market.

March 10: Mercury turns direct again.

March 11: Moon passes 90 degrees square to Mars. The ECB meets to discuss monetary policy.

March 17-18: Moon passes by co-ruler Mars and records its minimum declination at the same time. The FOMC is meeting at ths time too.

March 22-23: Moon passes by co-ruler Neptune.

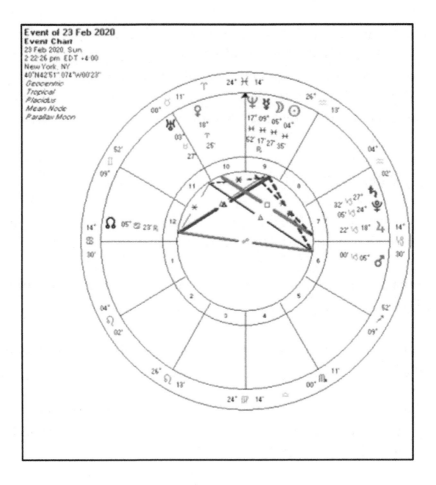

Figure 44
New Moon February 23, 2020

March – April 2020

Market action from late March through late April will be influenced by the New Moon cycle that commences on March 24 with Sun at 3 Aries. The horoscope in Figure 45 depicts planetary placements hours after the New Moon event as the Ascendant passes 14 Cancer. This lunar cycle runs until May 22.

This lunation has but one aspect to a planet of note. The lunation is within 4 degrees of exact conjunction to co-ruler Neptune. This portends an added measure of volatility during this lunar cycle.

Key dates to be alert to in this lunation include:

March 26; Moon makes a 90 degree square aspect to co-ruler Mars.

April 1: Moon passes the key 14 of Cancer point. Moon records its maximum declination at the same time. This duality of astro events portends added *volatility* plus a possible trend change.

April 8: Moon makes a 90 degree square to co-ruler Mars.

April 14: Moon records its minimum declination.

April 16: Moon transits past co-ruler Mars. Venus starts to make its approach to maximum declination.

April 19: Moon passes co-ruler Neptune.

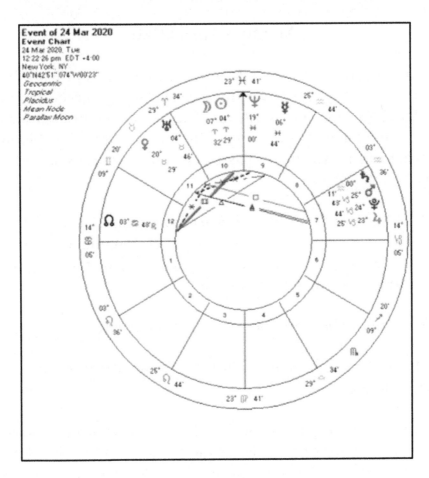

Figure 45
New Moon March 24, 2020

April - May 2020

Market action from late April through late May will be influenced by the New Moon cycle that commences on April 23 with Sun at 3 Taurus. The horoscope in Figure 46 depicts planetary placements hours before the New Moon event as the Ascendant passes 14 Cancer. This lunar cycle runs until May 22. This lunation is at a hard 90 degree square aspect to Saturn, Jupiter and arguably Pluto. At the same time, co-ruler Neptune is positioned within a handful of degrees from the NYSE natal mid-Heaven point. This all is suggestive of an energized cycle with plenty of added volatility.

Key dates to be alert to during this lunation include:

April 26: Moon passes 90 degrees square to Neptune.

April 28: Moon passes 14 of Cancer point as Moon makes its maximum declination.

April 28-30: Both the FOMC and the ECB meet over this span of time.

May 3: Venus at exact maximum declination.

May 7: Moon makes a 90 degree aspect to co-ruler Mars.

May 9: Moon makes a 90 degree aspect to co-ruler Neptune.

May 11: Moon at minimum declination.

May 13: Venus turns retrograde and remains so through

June 24. Venus retrograde periods usually deliver "action".

May 14-16: Moon transits past co-ruler Mars and then past co-ruler Neptune.

May 20: Venus has now completed its maximum declination event.

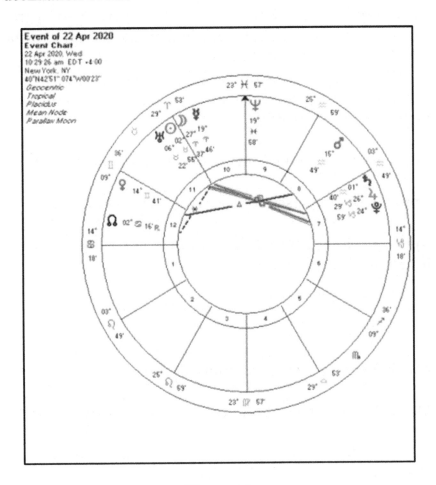

Figure 46
New Moon April 23, 2020

May-June 2020

Market action from late May through late June will be influenced by the New Moon cycle that commences on May 22 with Sun at 2 Gemini. The horoscope in Figure 47 depicts planetary placements hours before the New Moon event as the Ascendant passes 14 Cancer. This lunar cycle runs until June 21. This lunation is at a favorable 120 degree trine aspect to Saturn and Jupiter. Also important to remember, at this time heliocentric Jupiter and Saturn are within 9 degrees of each other. The Gann Master Cycle ending point is now in play. With each subsequent month, these two heavy-weights will draw nearer to one another. NYSE co-ruler Neptune is positioned within a handful of degrees from the NYSE natal mid-Heaven point. The lunation itself is within orb of being 90 degrees square to co-ruler Mars. This all is suggestive of an energized cycle with plenty of added volatility.

Key dates to be alert to during this lunation include:

May 25: Moon at maximum declination.

May 26: Moon transits past the 14 of Cancer point.

June 4 to 20: transiting co-ruler Mars makes a swweping 0 degree conjunction to co-ruler Neptune. This added energy coming amidst a Venus retrograde situation could translate into added volatility across equity markets.

June 4: ECB meets.

June 5: Moon makes a 90 degree hard aspect to both co-ruler plants, Mars and Neptune.

June 7: Moon at minimum declination.

June 9-10: FOMC meets.

June 13: Moon transits past co-ruling Mars and Neptune. This is a Saturday, so the effect may well be felt on the Friday. Mercury also turns retrograde on this date.

June 20: Moon passes at a 90 degree square aspect to both co-ruling planets.

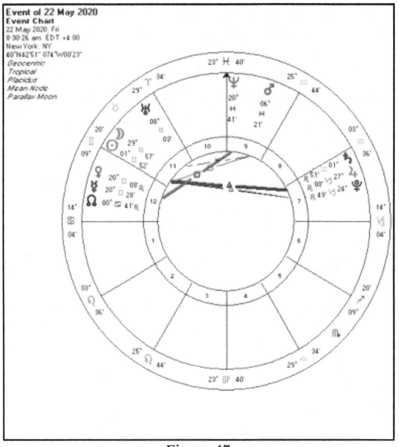

Figure 47
New Moon May 22, 2020

June-July 2020

Market action from late June through late July will be influenced by the New Moon cycle that commences on June 21 with Sun at 0 Cancer. The horoscope in Figure 48 depicts planetary placements hours before the New Moon event as the Ascendant passes 14 Cancer. This lunar cycle runs until July 20. NYSE co-ruler Neptune is positioned within a handful of degrees from the NYSE natal mid-Heaven point. But, so is co-ruler Mars. This concentration of energy portends a lunar cycle with added zest and volatility. Add to the mix the Mercury retrograde situation that lingers for the first part of this cycle, the ending of Venus retrograde and the start of Venus as the Morning Star and you have the recipe for a volatile time.

Key dates to be alert to during this lunation include:

June 22: Moon is at maximum declination as it transits past the critical 14 of Cancer point.

June 24: Venus retrograde is complete. Venus will start to be visible as the Morning Star.

July 3: Moon passes 90 degees square to Neptune.

July 5: Moon passes 90 degrees square to Mars and makes its minimum declination.

July 10-12: Moon transits past Mars and Neptune. This is a week-end, so watch for a market reaction on the Friday or the Monday. Mercury retrograde completes. The ECB meets in this timeframe too.

July 19: Moon at maximum declination as it passes 14 of

Cancer and makes a 90 degree square to co-ruler Mars. Watch for a market reaction on the Monday.

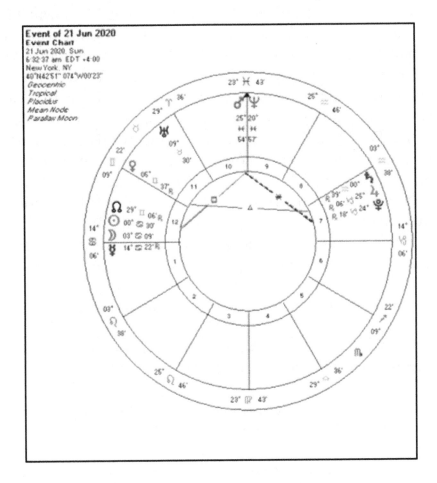

Figure 48
New Moon June 21, 2020

July-August 2020

Market action from late July through late August will be influenced by the New Moon cycle that commences on July 20 with Sun at 28 Cancer. The horoscope in Figure 49 depicts planetary placements hours before the New Moon event as the Ascendant passes 14 Cancer. This lunar cycle runs until August 19. NYSE co-ruler Neptune is positioned within a handful of degrees from the NYSE natal mid-Heaven point. The lunation is 120 degrees trine to this mid-Heaven point and opposite planetrary heavy-weights Jupiter, Saturn and Pluto.

Key dates to be alert to during this lunation include:

July 28-29: FOMC meets.

July 31: Moon passes 90 degrees square to Neptune.

August 1-2: Moon at minimum declination as it makes a 90 degree square to Mars.

August 6: Moon transits past Neptune and also the natal mid-Heaven point at 24 Pisces.

August 9: Moon passes Mars as ECB meets.

August 14: Moon at 90 degrees to Neptune.

August 16: Moon passes 14 of Cancer and makes a 90 degree square to Mars. This is a Sunday, so watch for a market reaction on the Monday. Moon is also at maximum declination at this date.

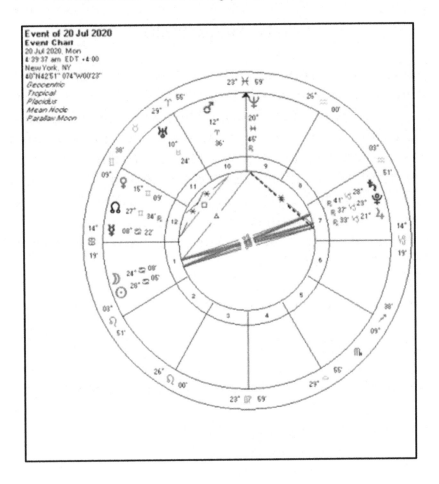

Figure 49
New Moon July 20, 2020

August-September 2020

Market action from late August through late September will be influenced by the New Moon cycle that commences on August 19 with Sun at 26 Leo. The horoscope in Figure 50 depicts planetary placements hours after the New Moon event as the Ascendant passes 14 Cancer. This lunar cycle runs until September 17. NYSE co-ruler Neptune is positioned within a handful of degrees from the NYSE natal mid-Heaven point. The lunation is 120 degrees trine to the other NYSE co-ruler Mars. Heliocentric Jupiter is now within 5 degrees of Saturn. The Master Cycle is nearing an exact conjunction.

Key dates to be alert to during this lunation include:

August 27: Moon transits 90 degrees to co-ruler Mars.

August 29: Moon is at minimum declination.

September 3: Moon transits past Neptune and the natal mid-Heaven point at 24 Pisces.

September 6: Moon passes co-ruler Mars.

September 9: Mars turns retrograde.

September 10: Moon moves past a 90 degree aspect to Neptune.

September 12-13: Moon passes 14 of Cancer and makes a 90 degree square to Mars. This is a week-end so watch for a reaction on the Monday. Moon also records its maximum declination.

September 15-16: FOMC meets.

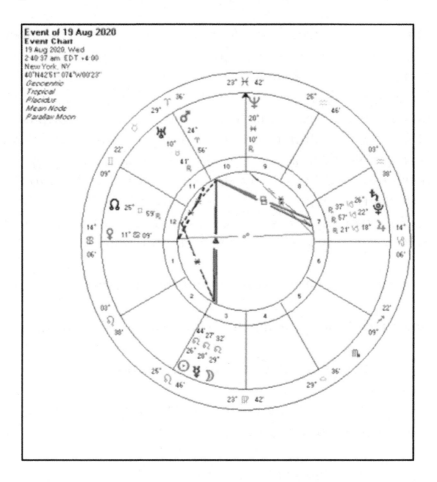

Figure 50
New Moon August 19, 2020

September - October 2020

Market action from late September through late October will be influenced by the New Moon cycle that commences on September 17 with Sun at 24 Virgo. The horoscope in Figure 51 depicts planetary placements hours before the New Moon event as the Ascendant passes 14 Cancer. This lunar cycle runs until October 16. NYSE co-ruler Neptune is positioned within a handful of degrees from the NYSE natal mid-Heaven point. The lunation is 180 degrees opposite to the natal mid-Heaven and to Neptune. Normally opposite aspects are not overly powerful, but this one deserves some attention with heliocentric Jupiter is now within 3 degrees of Saturn. The Master Cycle is nearing an exact conjunction.

Key dates to be alert to during this lunation include:

September 23: Moon at a 90 degree aspect to Neptune.

September 25-26: Moon at minimum declination as it makes a 90 degree square to Mars.

September 30: Moon passes Neptune.

October 1: Moon passes natal mid-Heaven point.

October 8: Moon passes 90 degrees to Neptune.

October 9: Moon passes over 14 of Cancer as it makes a 90 degree square to Mars and records its maximum declination.

October 14: Mercury turns retrograde.

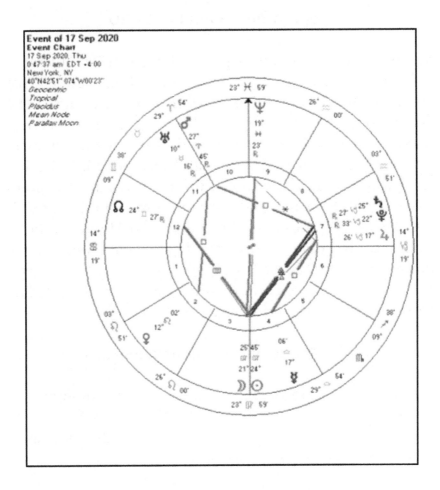

Figure 51
New Moon September 17, 2020

October - November 2020

Market action from late October through late November will be influenced by the New Moon cycle that commences on October 16 with Sun at 24 Libra. The horoscope in Figure 52 depicts planetary placements hours after the New Moon event as the Ascendant passes 14 Cancer. This lunar cycle runs until November 15. NYSE co-ruler Neptune is positioned within a handful of degrees from the NYSE natal mid-Heaven point. The lunation is 180 degrees opposite to co-ruler Mars. Normally opposite aspects are not overly powerful, but this one deserves some attention with heliocentric Jupiter is now within 1 degree of Saturn. The Master Cycle is at its exact conjunction.

Key dates to be alert to during this lunation include:

October 20: Moon passes 90 degrees to Neptune.

October 22: Moon at minimum declination as it makes a 90 degree aspect to Mars.

October 27: Moon passes Neptune and the natal mid-Heaven.

October 29: Moon passes Mars. ECB meets to discuss monetary matters.

November 2: Mercury retrograde completes.

November 4-5: FOMC meets.

November 5-6: Moon makes its maximum declination as it passes 14 of Cancer and makes a 90 degree aspect to

Mars.

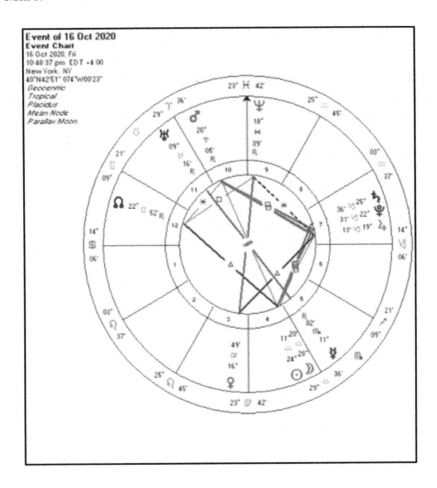

Figure 52
New Moon October 16, 2020

November - December 2020

Market action from late November through late December will be influenced by the New Moon cycle that commences on November 15 with Sun at 23 Scorpioa. The horoscope in Figure 53 depicts planetary placements hours before the New Moon event as the Ascendant passes 14 Cancer. This lunar cycle runs until December 14. NYSE co-ruler Neptune is positioned within a handful of degrees from the NYSE natal mid-Heaven point. The lunation is 120 degrees trine to co-ruler Neptune and the NYSE natal mid-Heaven point. Heliocentric Jupiter is now exact to Saturn. The Master Cycle is at its exact conjunction.

Key dates to be alert to during this lunation include:

November 14: Mars completes retrograde.

November 16: Moon is 90 degrees square to Neptune.

November 18: Moon at minimum declination as it squares co-ruler Mars.

November 23: Moon passes co-ruler Neptune and the natal mid-Heaven.

November 25: moon passes co-ruler Mars.

December 1: Moon passes 90 degrees to Neptune.

December 3-4: Moon at maximum declination as it squares Mars and passes 14 of Cancer.

December 10: ECB meets.

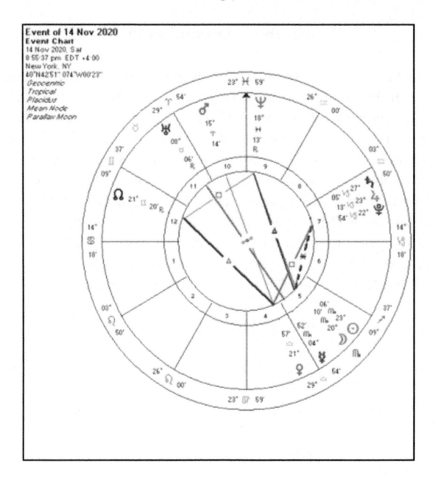

Figure 53
New Moon November 15, 2020

December 2020 - January 2021

Market action from late December through late January 2021 will be influenced by the New Moon cycle that commences on December 14 with Sun at 23 Sagittarius. The horoscope in Figure 54 depicts planetary placements hours after the New Moon event as the Ascendant passes 14 Cancer. This lunar cycle runs until January 13. NYSE co-ruler Neptune is positioned within a handful of degrees from the NYSE natal mid-Heaven point. The lunation is 90 degrees square to co-ruler Neptune and the NYSE natal mid-Heaven point. Heliocentric Jupiter is now 3 degrees separated from Saturn. The Master Cycle is beginning anew for the next 20 years.

Key dates to be alert to during the part of this lunar cycle leading into year end are:

December 15-16: FOMC meets.

December 16: Moon passes 90 degrees to Mars.

December 20-21: Moon passes Neptune and natal mid-Heaven point.

December 23: Moon passes co-ruler Mars.

December 28 - 31: Moon at maximum declination as it passes 14 of Cancer and makes a 90 degree square to Mars.

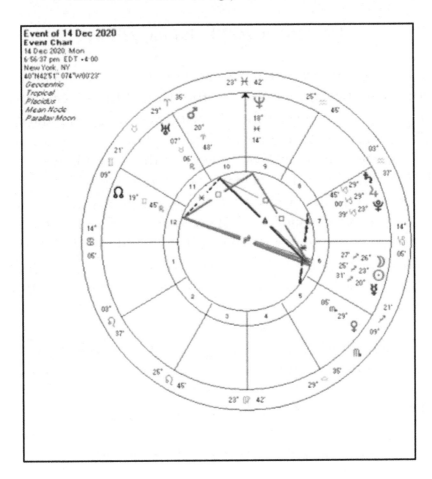

Figure 54
New Moon December 14, 2020

CHAPTER ELEVEN

Commodities 2020 Astrology

Gold

Investors who own Gold are accustomed to routinely checking the price of Gold by tuning into a television business channel or perhaps obtaining a live quote of Gold futures. What many do not realize is that Gold is a unique entity - for quietly working behind the scenes is an archaic methodology called the *London Gold Fix*.

The London Gold Fix occurs at 10:30 am and 3:00 pm local time each business day in London. Participants in the daily fixes are: Barclay's, HSBC, Scotia Mocatta (a division of Scotia Bank of Canada) and Societe Generale. These twice daily collaborations (some would say collusions) provide a benchmark price that is then used around the globe to settle and mark-to-market all the various Gold-related derivative contracts in existence.

The history of the Gold Fix is a fascinating one. On the 12th of September 1919, the Bank of England made arrangements with N.M. Rothschild & Sons for the formation of a Gold market in which there would be one official price for Gold quoted on any one day. At 11:00 am, the first Gold fixing took place, with the five principal gold bullion traders and refiners of the day present. These traders and refiners were N.M. Rothschild & Sons, Mocatta & Goldsmid, Pixley & Abell, Samuel Montagu & Co. and Sharps Wilkins.

The horoscope in Figure 55 depicts planetary positions at this date in history. Observations that jump off the page include: North Node had just changed signs, Venus was retrograde, Sun and Venus were conjunct, Mercury and Saturn were conjunct, Mars, Neptune and Jupiter were all conjunct at/near the Mid-Heaven point of the horoscope and Saturn was 180 degrees opposite Uranus.

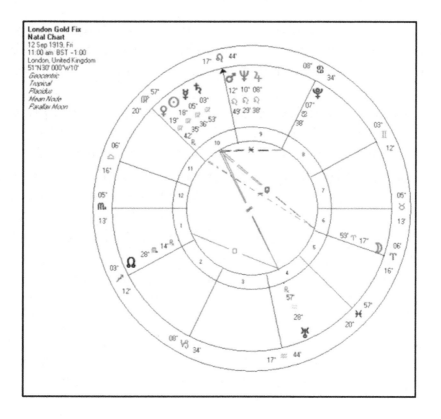

Figure 55
1919 London Gold Fix horoscope

Gold investors who have been around for a while will remember the significant $800/ounce price peak recorded by Gold in January 1980. To illustrate how astrology is linked to Gold prices, consider that at this price peak the transiting North Node had just changed signs and was 90 degrees hard aspect to the natal Node in the 1919 horoscope. Consider too that Mars and Jupiter were both coming into a 0 degree conjunction with the natal Sun location in the 1919 horoscope. For those who were involved in Gold more recently, recall that Gold hit a significant peak in early September 2011 at just over $1900/ounce. At that peak, Sun and Venus were conjunct to one another as they were in the 1919 Gold Fix horoscope. What's more, they were within a few degrees of being conjunct to the natal Sun location in the 1919 horoscope. A coincidence you say? I say not.

In the few weeks that followed this 2011 peak, Gold prices plunged nearly $400/ounce. But, then Gold found its legs again and began to rally. This rally seems directly related to Mars coming into a 0 degree conjunction to the Mars-Jupiter-Neptune location of the 1919 horoscope wheel.

Such is the complex nature of Gold prices. I have studied past charts of Gold and I am shocked at how many price inflection points are related in one way or another to the astrology of the 1919 Gold Fix horoscope wheel. To those readers who are of the opinion that Gold price is manipulated – your notion is indeed a valid one and it is my firm belief that astrology is the secret language being spoken amongst those that play a hand in the manipulation.

Gold futures contracts started trading in America on the New York Mercantile Exchange on December 31, 1974. Figure 56 illustrates the planetary positions in 1974 at the first trade date of Gold futures.

Note that in the 1919 chart Mars and Neptune are conjunct one another. Now, observe in Figure 56 that Mars and Neptune are also conjunct in the 1974 chart.

Next, ask yourself why the New York Mercantile Exchange would launch a new futures contract on December 31 – a time when most staff would be off for Christmas holidays. If this seems more than a bit odd, you are not alone in your thinking.

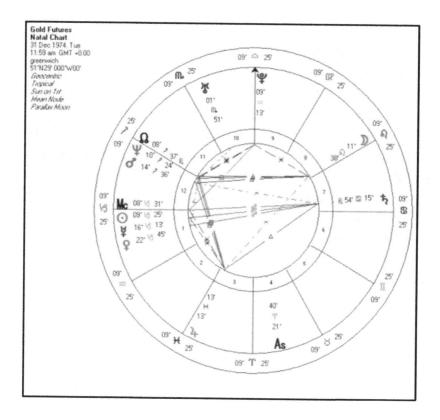

Figure 56
Gold futures First Trade horoscope

Take a look at the location of Moon in the 1974 horoscope. Moon is at 11 degrees of Leo. Now, take a look at the 1919 horoscope and observe that 11 degrees of Leo is where Mars and Neptune are located. I take these curious placements as further evidence of a deliberately timed astrological connection between Gold price, the 1919 Gold Fix date and the 1974 first trade date for Gold futures. All very intriguing stuff to be sure.

Transiting Mars/1974 natal Sun

Times when certain celestial objects transit past key points in the 1974 first trade horoscope deserve attention. One transiting body to consider is Mars. Transiting Mars passing the natal Sun location from the 1974 First Trade horoscope is a valuable tool for Gold traders to consider. Consider also the 90 and 180 degree aspects. The chart in Figure 57 has been overlaid with 0, 90 and 180 degree aspects of transiting Mars / natal Sun. Note how these events align to various inflection points on the price chart. In early 2019 a Mars/natal Sun square aspect sparked an $80 per ounce rally. This rally faded, but price action received another jolt that sparked a $200 rise as Mars passed 180 degrees to natal Sun.

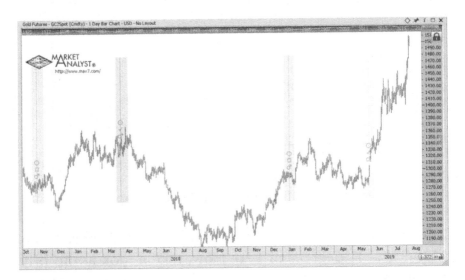

Figure 57
Transiting Mars / natal Sun aspects

For 2020, transiting Mars will make the following aspects to the 1974 natal Sun location:

Mid-February-mid-March: Mars slowly passes through a 0 degree conjunction to natal Sun.

July: Mars passes slowly through a 90 degree square to

natal Sun.

Transiting Sun and Mars /1919 natal Sun

Times when certain celestial objects transit past key points in the 1919 Gold fix horoscope also warrant attention. For 2020, transiting Sun will make the following aspects to the 1919 natal Sun location:

February 1-15: passing 180 degrees opposite to 1919 natal Sun

June 2-June 15: passing 90 degrees to 1919 natal Sun

September 2-September 19: passing 0 degrees conjunct to 1919 natal Sun

December 4-December 16: passing 90 degrees to 1919 natal Sun

For 2020, transiting Mars will make the following aspects to the 1919 natal Sun location:

April 15 - May 6: passing 180 degrees to 1919 natal Sun.

Sun Conjunct Venus

Another cue from the 1919 chart is the conjunction between Sun and Venus. Figure 58 illustrates the effect of Sun/Venus conjunctions on Gold prices in 2019 when Venus and Sun were conjunct from July 24 through about September 22. Sun and Venus will not be conjunct in 2020. But, in 2021 from mid-February through April, Sun and Venus will again be passing in a wide orb of conjunction.

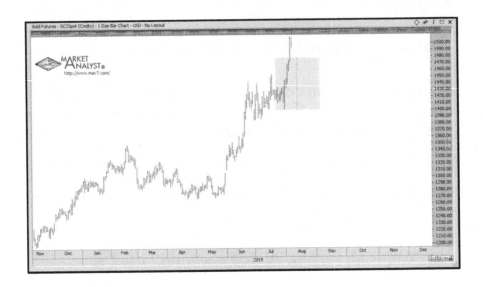

Figure 58
Sun conjunct Venus and Gold prices

Mercury Retrograde

Another valuable tool for Gold traders to consider is Mercury retrograde events. Watch for technical chart trend indictors to suggest a short term trend change at a retrograde event.

The chart in Figure 59 illustrates the connection between these Mercury phenomena and Gold prices. The correlation to swing highs and lows is rather striking.

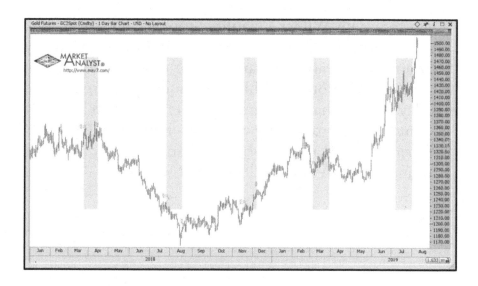

Figure 59
Mercury retrograde and Gold prices

For 2020, Mercury will be:
    retrograde from February 17 through March 9.
    retrograde from June 18 through July 11.
    retrograde from October 14 through November 2.

Reminder - Follow the Trend

At the risk of sounding overly repetitive, there is a piece of advice I wish to stress again. A question that I routinely get from those that follow my newsletter writings is – when during one of these astrological transit events should a person implement a trade? The answer is very simple. You should consider implementing a trade when you see the trend change. Always let the trend be your friend. I am sure you have heard this mantra before. I cannot emphasize it enough. There are many ways of measuring trend. My experience has shown me that the methodologies developed by J. Welles Wilder are very powerful for identifying trend changes. In particular I prefer to use his Wilder Volatility Stop. Wilder's 1978 book *New Concepts in Technical Trading Systems* is a highly recommended read if you are seeking to learn more about his methods. Another technique for gauging trend is to overlay a price chart with moving averages, such as the 34 day and 55 day ones. By the way, there are Fibonacci numbers and I routinely use them in my personal examination of trend.

Silver

Silver futures started trading on a recognized financial exchange in July 1933. Figure 60 shows the First Trade horoscope for Silver futures in geocentric format.

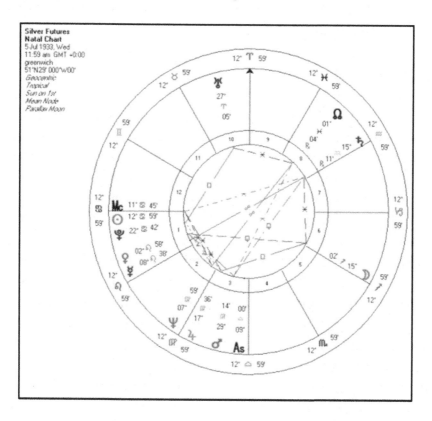

Figure 60
Silver futures First Trade horoscope

My research has shown that times when transiting Sun, transiting Mars and transiting Jupiter make hard aspects to the natal Sun point at 12 degrees Cancer should be watched carefully for evidence of trend changes and price inflection points. I am intrigued with this First Trade date. I suppose Silver could have started trading anytime in 1933. July 4, 1776 is a critical date in US history and on this date Sun was at 14 Cancer. Recall that 14 Cancer also figures prominently in the first trade horoscope of the NYSE. In 1933, markets would have been closed for the 4th of July celebrations. A first trade date of July 5, is as close as authorities could come to the July 4 date. On July 5, Sun at 12 degrees, 59 minutes is within a degree of the critical 14 of Cancer point.

Jupiter / natal Sun

In April 2011, Silver prices reached a peak at just under $50 per ounce. Transiting Jupiter was making a 90 degree aspect to natal Sun at the time. From this peak, Silver prices declined towards a significant low in late 2015. Along the way, transiting Jupiter made a 0 degree conjunction to natal Sun in the August 2013 timeframe. Silver prices behaved extremely erratically during this period. During October, November and December 2016, Jupiter made a 90 degree hard aspect to the natal Sun position. The price chart in Figure 61 illustrates this transit. Note that the start of this transit commenced with a sharp rally from $17 to $19/oz. Prices then collapsed to $15.50. The exact end of this collapse came just as the Jupiter transit wrapped up. Co-incidence you say? I say not. If these price moves appear small, remember a $1 move on Silver is $5000 per contract traded.

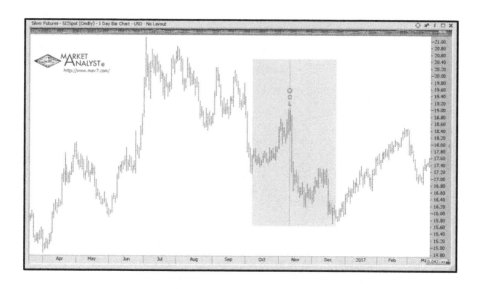

Figure 61
Silver futures and Jupiter / natal Sun

The next hard aspect of Jupiter to natal Sun (a 180 degree opposition) will occur in the January to early February timeframe of 2020 just as the Gann Master Cycle starts to come into focus.

Sun / natal Sun

The daily Silver price chart in Figure 62 has been overlaid with times when transiting Sun makes 0, 90 and 180 degree aspects to the natal Sun position at 12 Cancer. Note how these events bear a good alignment to price inflection points. Using a suitable measure of trend change (ie one of Wilder's methods), one would implement a trade during these Sun/natal Sun aspects if the trend recorded a change. Note that it is also possible for a Sun/natal Sun aspect to cause an existing trend to accelerate.

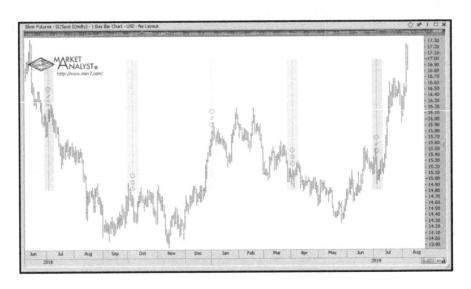

Figure 62
Silver and Sun/natal Sun events

For 2020, Sun will make aspects to natal Sun as follows:
December 27, 2018 – January 8, 2019: Sun 180 degrees to natal Sun.

March 25-April 7: Sun will pass 90 degrees to natal Sun.

June 26-July 10: Sun will pass 0 degrees to natal Sun.

September 28-October 10: Sun passes 90 degrees to natal Sun.

Mars / natal Sun

The Silver price chart in Figure 63 has been overlaid with times when transiting Mars makes 0, 90 and 180 degree aspects to the natal Sun position. Using a suitable measure of trend change (ie one of Wilder's methods), one would implement a trade during these Mars/natal Sun aspects if the trend recorded a change. Notice in this chart that the start of a push higher in price started just as a Mars conjunct natal Sun aspect was starting.

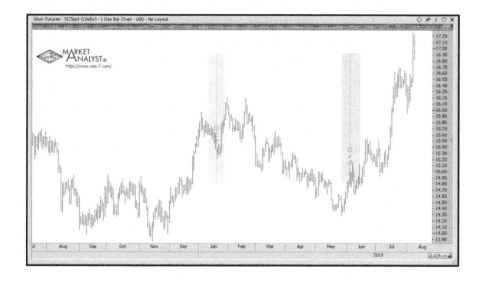

Figure 63
Silver and Mars/natal Sun events

For 2020, Mars will make aspects to natal Sun as follows:

February 26 – March 12: Mars will pass 180 degrees to natal Sun.

July 8 - 28: Mars will pass 90 degrees to natal Sun.

Declination

Planetary declinations should also be considered when studying price action of Silver futures. In particular the declination maxima and minima of Venus and also of Sun should be watched. Why Venus? As it turns out, Venus had just made its maximum declination in 1933 as Silver futures were starting to trade for the very first time. This is a very strong hint to me that Venus declination should be examined relative to Silver price inflections. Figures 70 and Figure 71 illustrate the effect of both Venus and Sun declination events. In 2018, Silver prices made what amounted to a double top formation at just over $17 in the April-June period which aligned with the beginning and end of a Venus declination maxima occurrence. The second of these tops aligned perfectly to the Sun at maximum declination (Summer Solstice). As maxima and minima in declination draw near, use a suitable trend change indicator to assist you in your decision making.

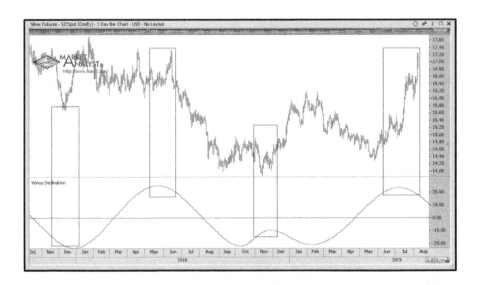

Figure 64
Venus Declination and Silver prices

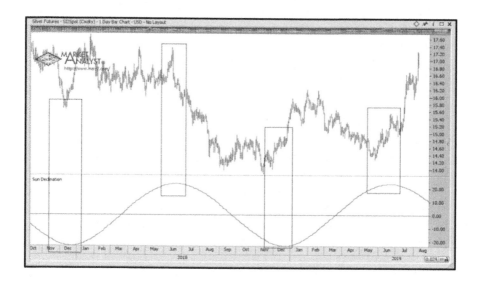

Figure 65
Sun Declination and Silver prices

For 2020, Sun will be at its maximum declination at the Summer Solstice on June 21. Sun will at its minimum declination at the Winter Solstice on December 21.

For 2020, Venus will exhibit its maximum declination from mid-April through mid-May.

It will be interesting to see how this factors in with the natal Sun location at 12 Cancer which falls right in the middle of this declination maxima event. Plus, this particular declination maxima sees Venus go *"out of bounds"*, meaning its declination is 27 degrees whereas a more normal maxima would be 23 degrees.

Copper

The First Trade Date for Copper futures was July 29, 1988. Figure 66 illustrates the First Trade horoscope in geocentric format.

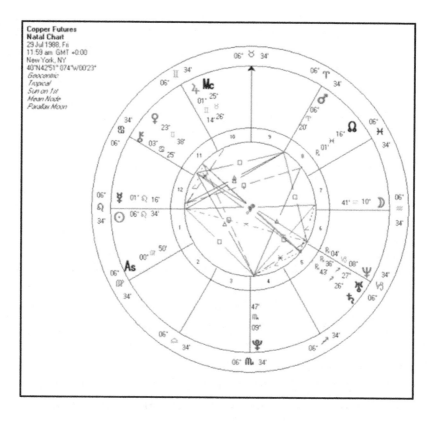

Figure 66

Copper futures First Trade horoscope

This horoscope wheel features an Inferior Conjunction of Mercury in the sign of Leo. Note also that Moon is in Aquarius. Recall from Chapter 1 that I noted during the Renaissance period, dreams were said to come true if Moon was in Aquarius. Whether this bit of arcane history factored into the selection of July 29, 1988 as the First

Trade date remains uncertain. But I would not be shocked to learn that there is a connection.

Also, notice in this horoscope that the First Trade date is that of a Full Moon.

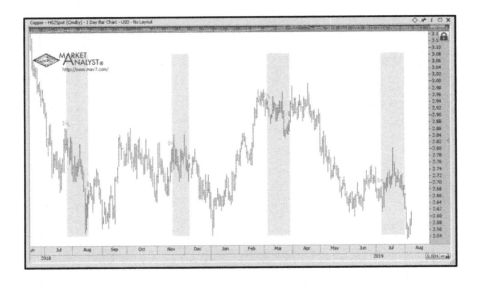

Figure 67
Copper and Mercury retrograde events

An Inferior Conjunction of Mercury marks the start of a new Mercury cycle around the Sun. Mercury Inferior Conjunction events always occur in association with Mercury being retrograde.

The daily price chart for Copper futures in Figure 67 has been overlaid with Mercury retrograde events. Knowing that such an event is approaching, one should watch a suitable price chart technical indicator for evidence of a short term trend change. Note that at the far right of this chart, Copper prices in mid-2019 took a steep dive during a retrograde occurrence.

For 2020, Mercury will be:

> retrograde from February 17 through March 9.
> retrograde from June 18 through July 11.
> retrograde from October 14 through November 2

As we move into 2020, I shall be watching Copper price action closely. I am seeing increasing evidence that mining companies in pursuit of Copper deposits are encountering geopolitical friction from foreign governments. This stands to negatively affect supply. Friction is also evident on the domestic front too. Canadian firm Hud Bay Minerals (TSX:HBM) has spent the past several years doing environmental background studies and engineering modelling studies on its planned Rosemont Copper project in Arizona. In mid-2019 the US Forest Service along with the US Army Corps of Engineers granted approval to Hud Bay to proceed with mine site development for what would have been the largest Copper mine in America. I say *would have* because without warning, out of the blue an Arizona court stripped Hud Bay of its permits and halted the entire project. It seems the judge sided with a group of environmentalists who were concerned about the mine site damaging the local flora and fauna. I suppose these people all live in houses with copper wiring and drive cars containing copper circuit wiring. But, a domestic Copper mine to ensure future supply at a reasonable price to promote economic growth? Apparently not.

Canadian Dollar, British Pound and Japanese Yen

These three futures instruments all started trading on May 16th, 1972 at the Chicago Mercantile Exchange. The horoscope in Figure 68 illustrates planetary placements at this date. It is interesting to note that Mars is 180 degrees opposite Jupiter. This suggests that Mars and Jupiter may play a role in price fluctuations on these currencies. Mars is also 0 degrees conjunct to Venus, suggesting another cyclical relationship.

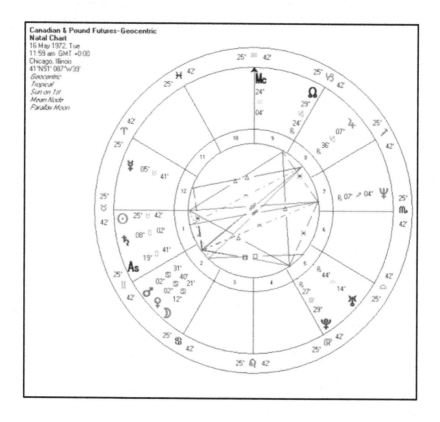

Figure 68
Pound, Yen, Canadian First Trade horoscope

The Mars Influence

The chart in Figure 69 illustrates price action on the Canadian Dollar. Mars conjunct Venus events only occur every couple years. As this chart shows, such an event occurred in early 2015 and as it did, the Canadian Dollar registered a low and a change of trend. Another conjunction in late 2015 resulted in an acceleration of the existing downward trend.

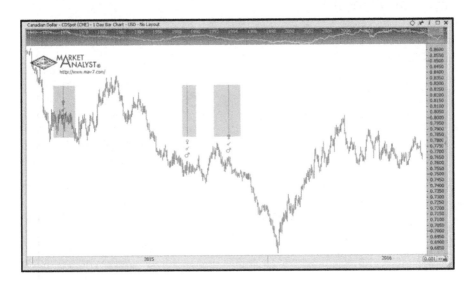

Figure 69
Canadian Dollar Mars conjunct Venus

The next such Mars/Venus event came in August 2019. Although not pictured here, the Canadian Dollar hit a high of nearly 77 cents in July, 2019. The trend then changed and fell to a low of under 75 cents in August where a sharp V-bottom was recorded right in the midst of the Mars/Venus conjunction. The next Mars/Venus conjunction will occur in mid-2021.

Natal Transits

Transiting Sun passing natal Sun, natal Mars and quite often natal Jupiter are events that currency traders may wish to focus on.

To illustrate, the chart in Figure 70 illustrates the effect on the British Pound of transiting Sun passing natal Mars (2 degrees of Cancer in the 1972 horoscope chart) and Sun passing natal Sun (25 of Taurus in the 1972 horoscope). Back in mid-2016 at the British Brexit Vote, the Pound took a drubbing and the plunge came right at a Sun / natal Mars conjunction. In Figure 70, a Sun passing natal Mars event in mid-2019 opened the floodgates for a steep fall in the Pound as Theresa May announced her resignation and Boris Johnson announced his intention to seek the Conservative Party leadtrership and the post of Prime Minister.

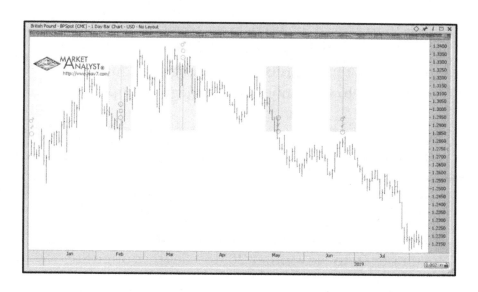

Figure 70
British Pound Sun passing natal Mars & natal Sun

Not every such transit aligns to such violent trend swings, but all such transits should be watched nonetheless.

In the waning days of the December 2019 British election, the Pound strengthened notably as Boris Johnson's campaign gathered momentum. As this was happening, Venus was transiting past natal Jupiter. On January 31, 2020 when Johnson is expected to pass the Brexit vote through the House of Commons, Venus will be at a favorable 72 degrees (5th harmonic) to natal Jupiter and a favorable 60 degrees to natal Sun.

The chart in Figure 71 illustrates the effect on the Canadian Dollar of transiting Sun passing natal Jupiter. The correlations are uncanny in their alignment.

For 2020, transiting Sun will make hard aspects to the natal Mars point of 2 degrees Cancer as follows:

March 16 to March 28: 90 degrees square
June 16 to June 29: 0 degrees conjunct
September 17 to September 30: 90 degrees square
December 16 to December 30: 180 degrees opposite

For 2020, transiting Sun will make hard aspects to the natal Sun point of 25 Taurus as follows:

February 7 to February 21: 90 degrees square
May 8 to May 24: 0 degrees conjunct
August 10 to August 27: 90 degrees square
November 10 to November 26: 180 degrees opposite

For 2020, transiting Sun will make hard aspects to the natal Jupiter point of 7 degrees Capricorn as follows:

March 20 to April 2: 90 degrees square
June 21 to July 5: 10 degrees opposite
September 22 to October 7: 90 degrees square
December 21 to January 4, 2020: 0 degrees conjunct

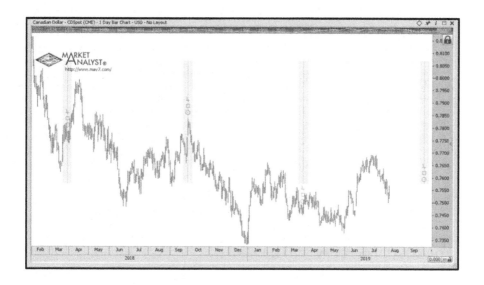

Figure 71
Canadian Dollar Sun conjunct natal Jupiter

Mercury Retrograde

Currency traders should pay close attention to Mercury retrograde events as they can bear a good alignment to trend changes on the Pound, Yen and Canadian Dollar.

The Canadian Dollar price chart in Figure 72 has been overlaid with Mercury retrograde events. Traders are advised to use a suitable trend change chart indicator to watch for actionable trend changes during retrograde events.

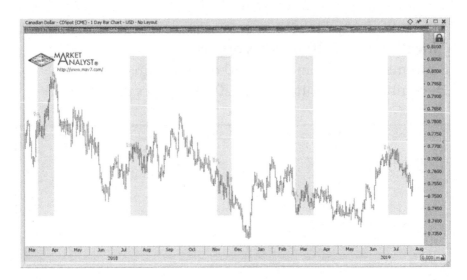

Figure 72
Canadian Dollar and Mercury retrograde

For 2020, Mercury will be:

> retrograde from February 17 through March 9.
> retrograde from June 18 through July 11.
> retrograde from October 14 through November 2

Euro Currency Futures

The Euro became the official currency for the European Union on January 1, 2002 when Euro bank notes became freely and widely circulated. Arguably there may be another date – January 1999 when the E.U. zone nations were required to establish a fixed rate of exchange between their currencies and the Euro currency.

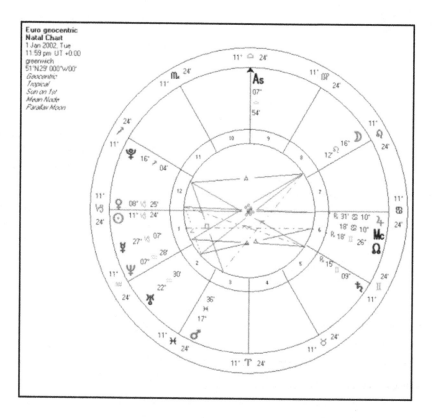

Figure 73
Euro Currency First Trade horoscope

But, I prefer the 2002 date because of the conjunct relation between Venus and Sun. The First Trade horoscope for the 2002 date in Figure 73 shows Sun and Venus are conjunct in Capricorn.

The chart of the Euro currency in Figure 74 has been overlaid with a recent Venus / Sun conjunct event. Note that the downtrend put on a second wave a decline during this event. More interestring is how the downtrend found a bottom just as this aspect completed itself. The next Sun Venus conjunction occurs in 2021.

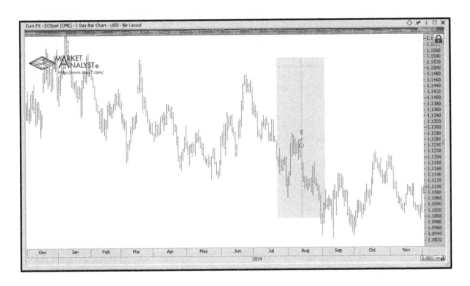

Figure 74
Sun / Venus Conjunction and the Euro

Natal Transits

Events of transiting Sun making 0, 90 and 180 degree aspects to the natal Sun position in the Euro 2002 First Trade horoscope are also worth watching as they often align to inflection points on the Euro. In 2019 notice how these transits all came within close proximity to price inflection points.

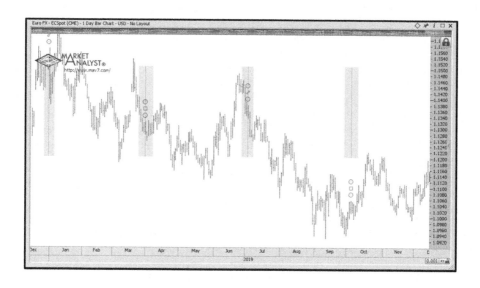

Figure 75
Natal Transits and the Euro Currency

For 2020, transiting Sun will be completing a 0 degree conjunction to natal Sun during the first week of January.

90 degrees to natal Sun March 26 through April 7.

180 degrees opposite natal Sun from June 22 through July 12.

90 degrees to natal Sun from 28 of September through October 9.

Australian Dollar

Australian dollar futures started trading on the Chicago Mercantile Exchange on January 13, 1987. As the horoscope in Figure 76 shows, Sun and Mercury are at Superior Conjunction at 22-23 degrees Capricorn.

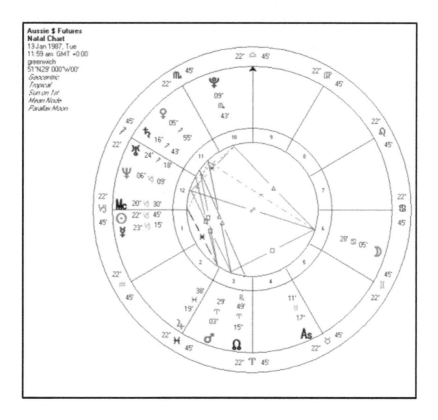

Figure 76
First Trade horoscope of Australian Dollar futures

Mercury Retrograde

Times when Mercury is retrograde should be considered when trading Australian Dollar futures. The chart in Figure 77 has been overlaid with Mercury retrograde events. These events often align to price inflection points.

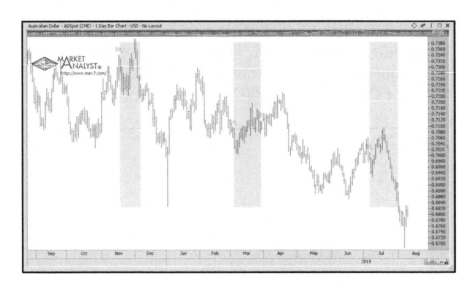

Figure 77
Australian Dollar and Mercury Conjunctions

For 2020, Mercury will be:

> retrograde from February 17 through March 9.
> retrograde from June 18 through July 11.
> retrograde from October 14 through November 2.

Natal Transits

Transits to the natal Sun position of 22 Capricorn from the 1987 First Trade horoscope can be used as tools to help one navigate the price action of the Australian Dollar as the price chart in Figure 78 illustrates. Most recently, transiting Sun making a 180 degree opposition to natal Sun was a precursor to a substantial decline in the value of the currency.

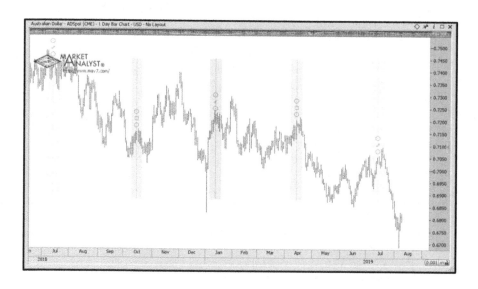

Figure 78
Australian Dollar and Sun/natal Sun events

For 2020, transiting Sun will make 0, 90, and 180 degree aspects to natal Sun:

0 degrees to natal Sun from January 5 through January 21

90 degrees square to natal Sun from April 6-18th.

180 degrees to natal Sun from July 6 through July 25

90 degrees to natal Sun from October 9 through October 21.

30 Year Bond Futures

30 Year Bond futures started trading in Chicago on August 22, 1977. Figure 79 presents the geocentric First Trade horoscope for this date.

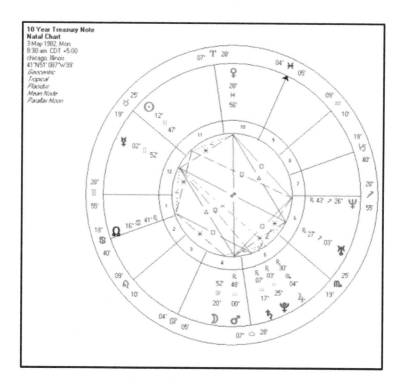

Figure 79
First Trade horoscope for 30 Year Bond futures

Natal Transits

My research has indicated that events of transiting Sun making 0, 90 and 180 degree aspects to the natal Jupiter position at 0 degrees Cancer are valuable tools for the Bond trader. Traders of the 30 Year Bond futures may wish to incorporate this information with a suitable technical trend indicator into their trades. Figure 80 illustrates Bond price performance with the Sun/natal Jupiter transits overlaid.

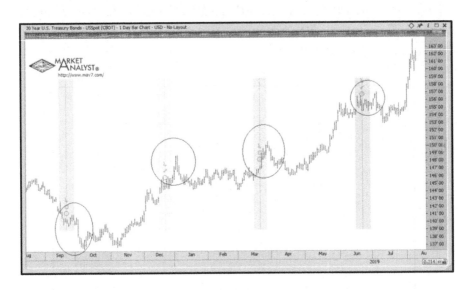

Figure 80
Bonds (30 Year) and Sun in aspect to natal Jupiter

For 2020, transiting Sun will make hard 0, 90 or 180 degree aspects to natal Jupiter as follows:

At January 1, a 180 degree aspect will just be wrapping up. Given the current strong uptrend, a reversion to the mean would not be out of the question in the coming Sun/natal Jupiter transit.

March 14 through March 29, transiting Sun will make a 90 degree aspect.

June 12 through July 1, transiting Sun will make a 0 degree aspect.

September 17 through September 30, transiting Sun will make a 90 degree aspect.

December 14 through December 29, transiting Sun will be completing a 180 degree hard aspect.

Mercury Retrograde

Look closely at the First Trade horoscope in Figure 79 and you will note that the position of Mercury (at 20 Virgo) is further delineated by a letter S. This letter denotes stationary and curiously enough this First Trade date of August 22, 1977 comes one day prior to Mercury turning retrograde. Therein rests a strong hint. The price chart in Figure 81 has been overlaid with Mercury retrograde events. Note the propensity for short term inflections in trend at these retrograde events.

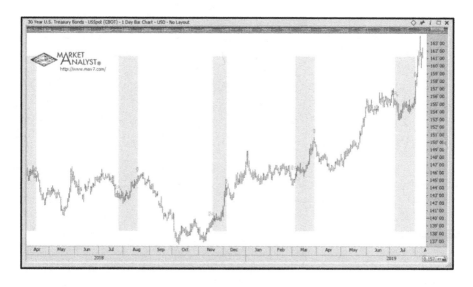

Figure 81
30 Year Bonds and Mercury retrograde

For 2020, Mercury will be:

retrograde from February 17 through March 9.

retrograde from June 18 through July 11.
retrograde from October 14 through November 2.

10 Year Treasury Note Futures

10 Year Treasury Notes started trading in Chicago on May 3, 1982. Figure 82 presents the geocentric First Trade horoscope for this date.

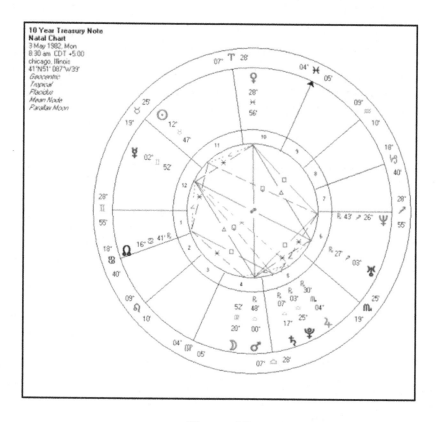

Figure 82
First Trade horoscope for 10 Year Treasury Notes

Retrograde

Notice in the First Trade horoscope in Figure 82, that Mars is denoted Rx which stands for retrograde. Therein rests another valuable clue. Figure 83 illustrates what happened in 2018 at a Mars retrograde event. The end of the retrograde period saw a trend change and the price of Treasury Notes decline. Mars will be retrograde from early September through to mid-November 2020.

Mercury retrograde events also bear watching when following price action on the 10 Year Treasury Notes. Figure 84 illustrates the connection between price inflection points and Mercury retrograde. Most recently, the retrograde event in July marked a sharp push higher as a flight to safety took place following China being labelled a currency manipulator.

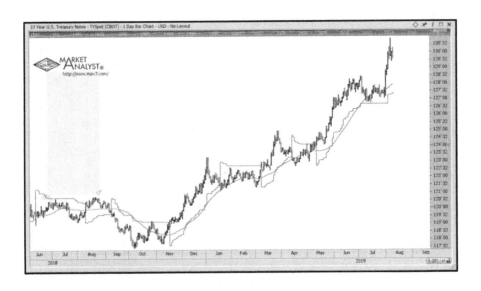

Figure 83
Mars retrograde and 10 Year Treasuries

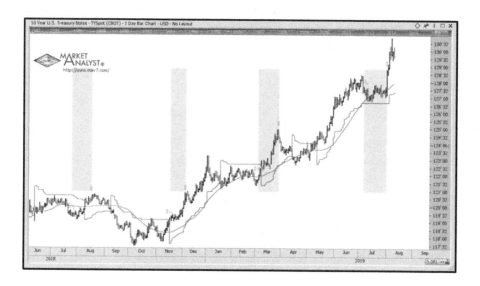

Figure 84
Mercury retrograde and 10 Year Treasuries

For 2020, Mercury will be:

retrograde from February 17 through March 9.
retrograde from June 18 through July 11.
retrograde from October 14 through November 2.

Wheat, Corn, Oats

Wheat, Corn and Oats futures all share the same first trade date from 1877. The horoscope in Figure 85 shows planetary placements at this date.

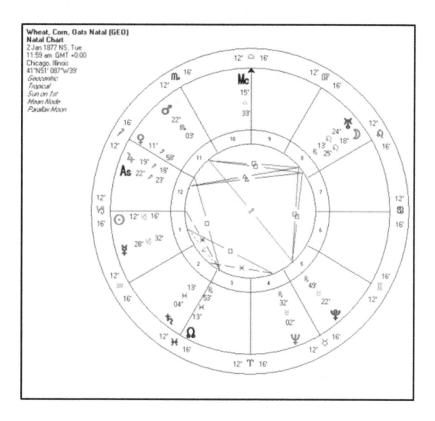

Figure 85
First Trade horoscope for Wheat, Corn and Oats futures

Over the past couple years, my reading and research has revealed that W.D. Gann was also known to follow a First Trade horoscope wheel from April 3, 1848, the date the Chicago Board of Trade was founded. Figure 86 shows this horoscope wheel.

In the 1877 Wheat/Corn natal horoscope, the Sun is at 12

Capricorn, exactly square to the location of Sun in the above shown 1848 horoscope.

In the 1877 chart, the Descendant is at 12 Cancer. Look where Jupiter is in this 1848 chart – within 0.5 degrees of 12 Cancer. Co-incidence you say? I rather doubt it.

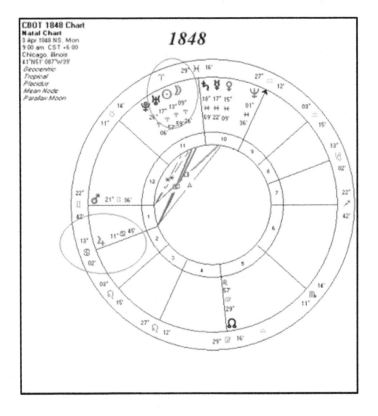

Figure 86
1848 First Trade horoscope for CBOT

Natal Aspects to Both Horoscopes

Events of transiting Sun making 0, 90 and 180 degree aspects to the natal Sun position in the 1877 First Trade horoscope or the 1848 CBOT natal horoscope can be used as a tool to guide traders through the price volatility of

Wheat, Corn and Oats. Because of the peculiar alignment of these two horoscopes, a 0 degree conjunction to natal Sun in the 1877 horoscope will be a 90 degree square to the natal Sun of the 1848 horoscope.

Figure 87 illustrates the effect on Corn prices of transiting Sun making hard aspects to the natal Sun position. Note how the significant low in mid-2018 came right at a Sun / natal Sun aspect.

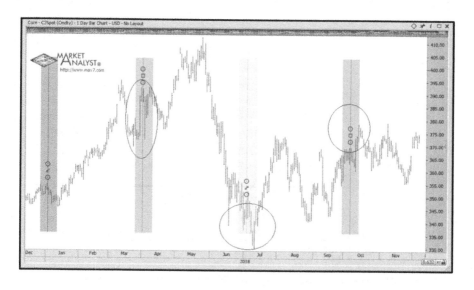

Figure 87
Corn prices and Sun/natal Sun events

In early 2019, the Sun conjunct natal Sun event marked a trend change and what would be a 40 cent per bushel price decline.

Mars is also a planet to keep tabs on. The application of a chart technical indicator to monitor short term trend changes is essential to properly utilizing these natal transits. In mid-2017 a Mars / natal Sun transit was within days of aligning to a significant price reversal point. In late 2017 a Mars / natal Sun aspect marked a floor of support. In April 2018 price reacted erratically during the transit. Figure 88 illustrates transiting Mars making hard aspects to the natal Sun position. A price peak occurred at the very end of a Mars natal Sun aspect in June 2019.

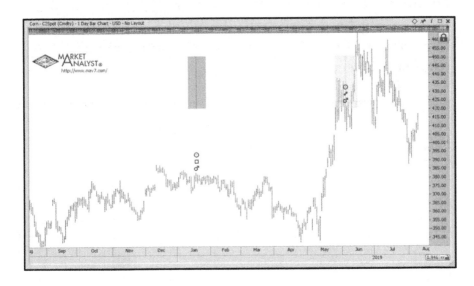

Figure 88
Corn prices and Mars/natal Sun events

For 2020, transiting Sun will be 0 degree to the 1877 natal Sun from January 1 through January 8. (90 degrees to the 1848 natal Sun).

Sun will be 90 degrees natal Sun from March 27 through April 8. (0 degrees to the 1848 natal Sun).

Sun will be 180 degrees natal Sun from June 26 through July 11. (90 degrees to the 1848 natal Sun).

Sun will be 90 degrees natal Sun from September 29 through October 11. (180 degrees to the 1848 natal Sun)

For 2020, Mars will be 0 degrees to the 1877 natal Sun from February 26 through the 13th of March. (90 degrees to the 1848 horoscope).

Mars will be 90 degrees to the 1877 natal Sun from July 8 through August 1.

Declination

Planetary declination also is a powerful tool that can be used to help traders identify the coming of trend reversals. Figures 89 and 90 illustrate the application of declination to Corn and Wheat price charts. If price has been rising (falling) and appears to be reaching what could be deemed an overbought (oversold) situation, check the declination level of Venus. If the declination is reaching an extreme or about to cross the zero level, you may find a trend reversal will soon make an appearance. A sizeable price rally on Corn got underway in May 2019 as Mars made its maximum declination. The zero declination point aligned to a price peal on Wheat in 2018 and a signific ant price low in April 2019.

For 2020, Venus will exhibit its maximum declination from mid-April through mid-May. In late December, Venus will be on its way to recording its minimum declination in early 2021. Zero declination will occur early February and early November. Mars will be at minimum declination in the latter part of February 2020.

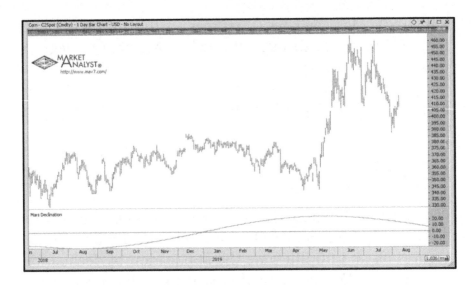

Figure 89
Corn prices and Mars Declination

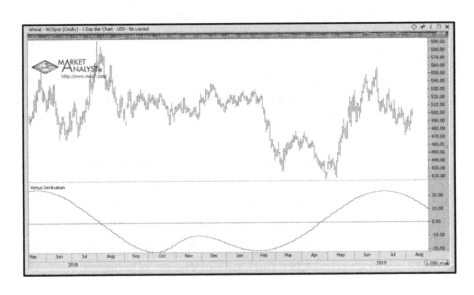

Figure 90
Wheat prices and Venus declination

Retrograde

My research has also shown that Mercury retrograde plays a role in price pivot points on the grains. The price chart of Wheat futures in Figure 91 has been overlaid with Mercury retrograde events. Not all retrograde events will automatically align to a trend change. The propensity for such trend changes are however significant. The use of a suitable chart technical indicator is strongly recommended. Although not shown here, Mercury retrograde events do have a similar propensity to align to trend changes on Corn prices.

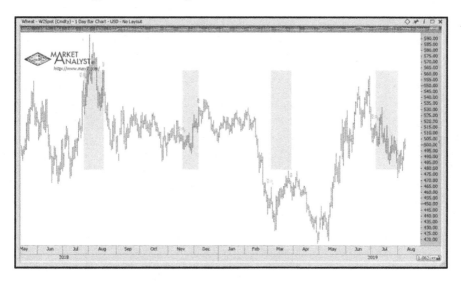

Figure 91
Wheat prices and Mercury retrograde events

For 2020, Mercury will be:

retrograde from February 17 through March 9.
retrograde from June 18 through July 11.
retrograde from October 14 through November 2.

Soybeans

Soybean futures started trading in Chicago on October 5, 1936. The horoscope in Figure 92 illustrates the planetary placements at that time. What I find intriguing is the location of the Sun. Notice how it is exactly 90 degrees to the location of the Sun in the First Trade horoscope for Wheat, Corn and Oats? Notice Sun is 180 degrees from the Sun in the 1848 CBOT natal chart? As I have previously suggested, the regulatory officials who determined these First Trade dates knew more about astrology than you may think.

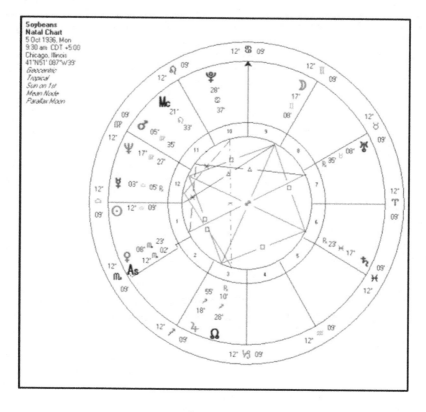

Figure 92
Soybeans First Trade horoscope

Natal Transits

Events of transiting Sun making 0, 90 and 180 degree aspects to the natal Sun position in the 1936 First Trade horoscope can be used to navigate the volatility of the Soybean market. Figure 93 illustrates the effect of transiting Sun making hard aspects to the natal Sun position. Figure 94 illustrates the effect of Mars making aspects to the natal Sun location. What I find intriguing is that the precipitous plunge in prices with the onset of the China trade spat started just as Venus was transiting 90 degrees to the natal Soybean Sun location.

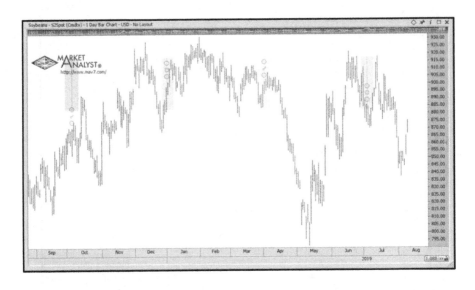

Figure 93
Soybeans and Sun/natal Sun events

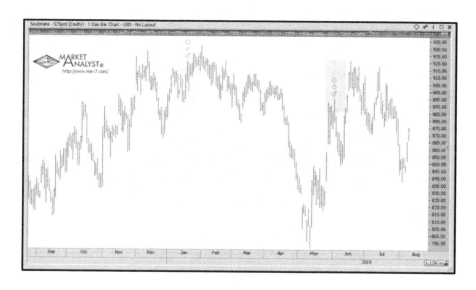

Figure 94
Soybeans and Mars/natal Sun events

For 2020, transiting Sun will make a 90 degree aspect to natal Sun from January 1 through January 8.

Transiting Sun will make a 180 degree aspect to natal Sun from March 25 through April 8.

A 90 degree aspect to natal Sun will occur from June 28 through July 11.

A 0 degree aspect will occur from September 26 through October 12.

For 2020, Mars will be 90 degrees to the 1936 natal Sun February 26 through the 13th of March.

Mars will be 180 degrees to the 1936 natal Sun from July 8 through August 1.

Retrograde

Mercury retrograde events also contribute to the price behavior of Soybeans. The Soybeans chart in Figure 95 illustrates the Mercury retrograde effect. If there is a trend change associated with Mercury retrograde, the trend change may come immediately beforehand, during or immediately afterwards. The use of a suitable chart technical indicator is essential to help identify the trend shifts.

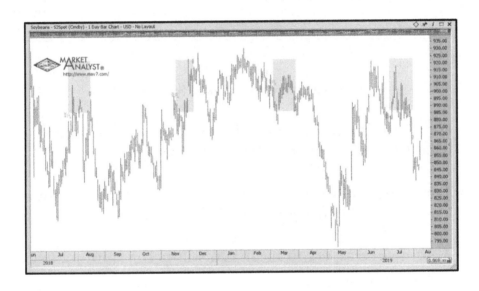

Figure 95
Soybeans and Mercury events

For 2020, Mercury will be:

retrograde from February 17 through March 9.
retrograde from June 18 through July 11.
retrograde from October 14 through November 2.

Declination

Soybeans also have a tendency to record price trend changes in proximity to Venus recording maximum, zero and minimum declinations. The Soybean price chart in Figure 96 illustrates further. Note that the 2018 precipitous China trade-war fueled sell-off got underway right at the declination maxima in early June of 2018. The two declination minima points in late 2018 and early 2019 aligned to trend reversals. A zero declination point in April 2019 saw a sisnificant price decline. The declination maxima in June 2019 aligned to a double top situation.

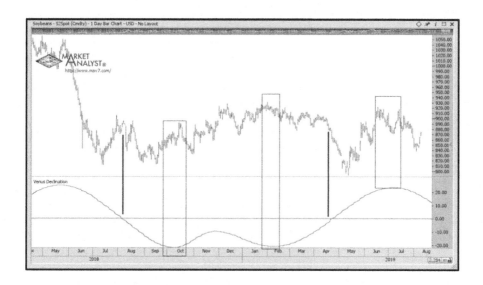

Figure 96
Soybeans and Venus Declination

For 2020, Venus will exhibit its maximum declination from mid-April through mid-May. In late December, Venus will be on its way to recording its minimum declination in early 2021. Zero declination will occur early February and early November.

Crude Oil

West Texas Intermediate Crude Oil futures started trading on a recognized exchange for the first time on March 30, 1983. A unique alignment of celestial points can be seen in the horoscope in Figure 97. Notice how Mars, North Node, (Saturn/Pluto/Moon) and Neptune conspire to form a rectangle.

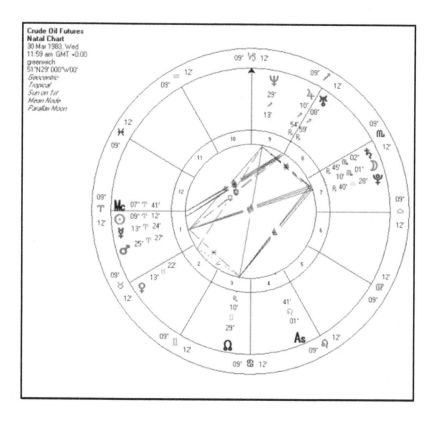

Figure 97
Crude Oil First Trade horoscope

Natal Transits

My experience has shown that Crude Oil is a complex instrument to analyze using astrology. Given the peculiar rectangular shape that appears in the horoscope, my strategy for analyzing Crude Oil has been to use natal transits with a focus on transiting Sun and transiting Mars making 0 degree aspects to the four corner points of the rectangle.

The chart in Figure 98 illustrates Oil price action with events of Mars transiting the corners of the peculiar horoscope rectangle. What is not shown on the chart is that the frightening lows of early 2016 came as Mars was passing the rectangle point denoted by Saturn/Moon. In 2019, Mars passing the natal Mars corner of the rectangle created a $4 per barrel price dip. In May 2019, Mars passing the Node corner of the rectangle resulted in a more substantive $14 drawdown in price.

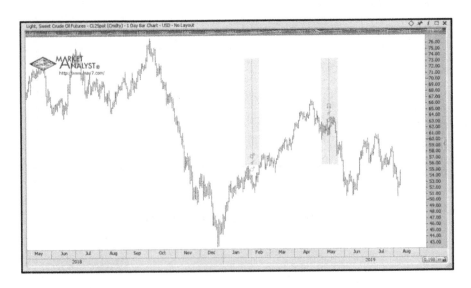

Figure 98
Crude Oil and Mars transits

Figure 99 illustrates events of Sun passing the rectangle corner positions in 2019 to date. A key reversal in price at the $42 level came in December 2018 as Sun passes the Neptune corner of the rectangle. A price high and trend change came in April 2019 at $66 as Sun passed the Mars corner of the rectangle. A price low at $51 in June came as Sun passed the Node corner of the rectangle. The alignment of these Sun transits to swings and trend changes is remarkable.

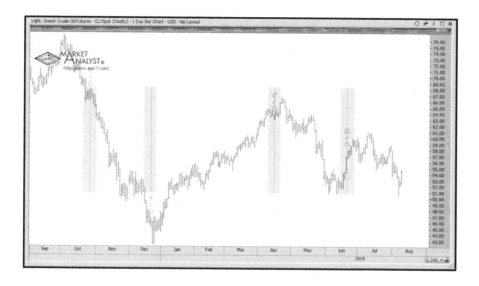

Figure 99
Crude Oil and Sun transits

For 2020, the four corners of the peculiar rectangle will be passed by as follows:

Sun will transit 0 degrees to the natal Mars location from April 9 through April 22.

Sun will transit 0 degrees to the natal Node location from June 7 through June 22.

Sun will transit 0 degrees to the natal (Saturn/Pluto/Moon) location from October 18 through November 1.

Sun will transit 0 degrees to the natal Neptune location from December 14 through the end of the year.

Mars will transit past the natal Neptune location between the 8th and 24th of February.

Mars will transit past the natal Mars location between August 6th and September 4th.

Retrograde

Crude Oil is influenced by Mercury retrograde and Venus retrograde. The Crude Oil price charts in Figure 100 and 101 illustrate this effect.

Figure 100
Crude Oil and Mercury retrograde events

At thus time of writing, Crude Oil is experiencing a period of weakness. This weakness started with a trend change at a Mercury retrograde event in July.

For 2020, Mercury will be:

> retrograde from February 17 through March 9.
> retrograde from June 18 through July 11.
> retrograde from October 14 through November 2.

Figure 101
Crude Oil and Venus retrograde events

Note from the chart in Figure 101, Oil prices hit a swing high in September 2018 in the $76 range. A Venus retrograde event then tied directly to a trend change and Oil prices fell substantially. For 2020, Venus will be retrograde May 13 through June 24. Pay strict attention to this period of time for possible drama on the Crude Oil front.

Cotton

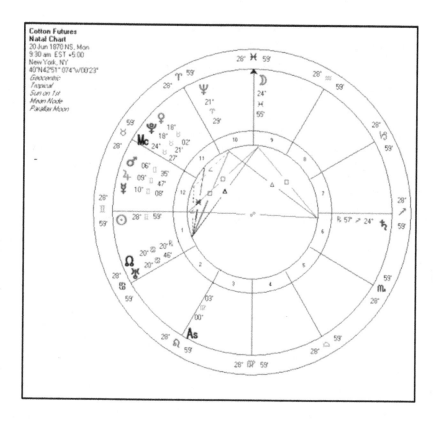

Figure 102
Cotton futures First Trade horoscope

After much painstaking research sifting through back-editions of New York newspapers, I have come to conclude that Cotton futures first started trading on June 20, 1870. The horoscope wheel in Figure 102 illustrates planetary placements at that time. At first glance, I find it peculiar that the Moon is at the same degree and sign location (24 Pisces) as is the Mid-Heaven in the New York Stock Exchange natal horoscope wheel from 1792. Surely this is no accident.

Natal Transits

Events of transiting Sun passing 0, 90 or 180 degrees to the natal Sun position are an effective tool for traders to use when navigating the choppy waters of Cotton prices. A suitable chart technical trend indicator is also a must. The Cotton price chart in Figure 103 illustrates further. Cotton prices at thus time of writing are continuing a grinding downtrend. Sun natal Sun transits have not been as accurate as in years past, as there has nit been a significant change of trend.

Figure 103
Cotton futures and Sun/natal Sun aspects

In 2020, transiting Sun will aspect natal Sun as follows:

Transiting Sun will pass 90 degrees to natal Sun from March 7 through March 23.

Transiting Sun will pass 0 degrees conjunct to natal Sun from June 10 through June 30.

Transiting Sun will pass 90 degrees to natal Sun from September 13 through September 30.

Transiting Sun will pass 180 degrees to natal Sun from December 12 through December 28.

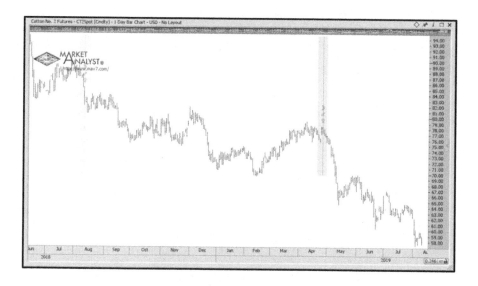

Figure 104
Cotton futures and Venus/natal Moon aspects

One other astro phenomenon traders may wish to consider as a tool to use is the occurrence of Venus passing by the natal Moon position at 24 Pisces.

Not a frequent event, it is nonetheless one to pay attention to. The price chart in Figure 104 illustrates.

In April 2019, a rally failed at a Venus natal Moon transit event. Cotton prices have subsequently declined 16 cents as at this time of writing.

During 2020, Venus will transit past the natal Moon from

late January through early February.

Coffee

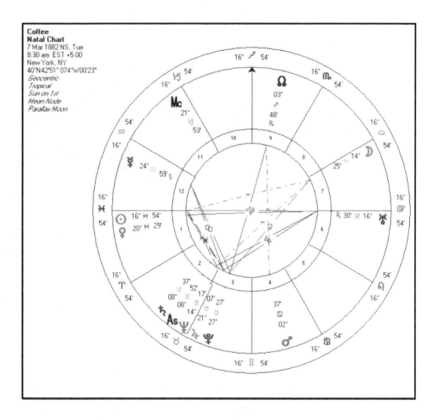

Figure 105
Coffee futures First Trade horoscope

Coffee futures started trading in New York in early March of 1882. The horoscope wheel in Figure 105 illustrates planetary placements at that time.

Natal Transits

In the Coffee horoscope, note the 180 degree aspect between Sun and Uranus. Louise McWhirter in her 1937 writings cautioned it is not wise to invest in situations where this sort of aspect exists because one will experience many wild ups and downs in price over time. A quick look at a 10 year price chart of Coffee reveals a price range of $0.65/pound to $3.06/pound with many wild swings. Point taken, Ms. McWhirter.

The Coffee price chart in Figure 106 has been overlaid with events of transiting Sun making 0, 90 and 180 degree aspects to the natal Sun position at 16 Pisces.

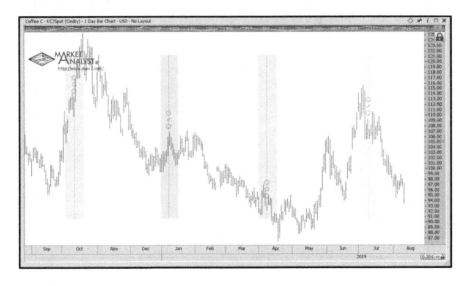

Figure 106

Coffee prices and natal transits

In 2020, transiting Sun will aspect natal Sun as follows:

Transiting Sun will pass 0 degrees conjunct to natal Sun from February 29 through March 16.

Transiting Sun will pass 90 degrees conjunct to natal Sun from May 31 through June 17.

Transiting Sun will pass 180 degrees to natal Sun from August 31 through September 19.

Transiting Sun will pass 90 degrees to natal Sun from December 10 through December 16.

non-Natal Transits

The positioning of Sun opposite Uranus in the 1882 natal horoscope is intrigiung. It turns out that real time 0, 90 and 180 degree aspects between Sun and Uranus can be used to further assist the Coffee trader with decision making.

In 2018 a key reversal in early May came mere days after a conjunction event and another reversal came in October at an opposition event. The subsequent downtrend endured right until April 2019.

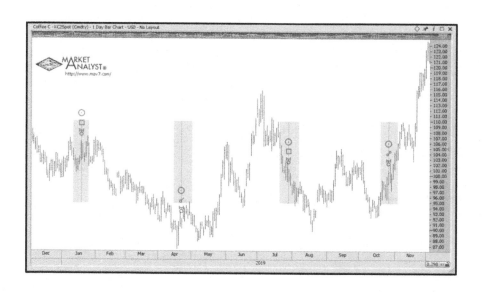

Figure 107

Coffee prices and Sun/Uranus aspects

These aspects between Sun and Uranus will sometimes fall just shy of the actual price turning point, but they do seem to be ominous nonetheless. Figure 107 illustrates recent aspects.

For 2020, Sun will make the following hard aspects (0, 90, 180 degree) with Uranus:

90 degrees from mid to late January.

0 degrees from mid to late April.

90 degrees from late July through August 10.

180 degrees from late October through early November.

Sugar

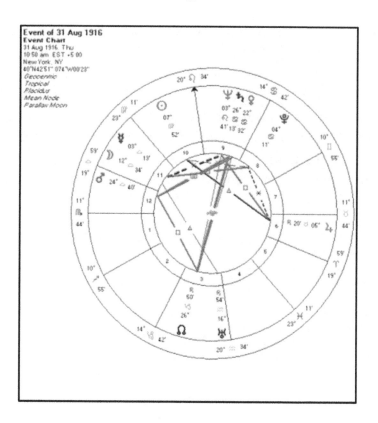

Figure 108
Sugar Futures First Trade horoscope

Sugar as a bulk commodity started trading in New York as early as 1881. My combing through old editions of New York newspapers suggests that in September 1914 there were plans to open a formal Sugar Exchange, but these plans were scuttled by World War 1. I am led to understand that a formal Exchange did open on August 31, 1916. The horoscope wheel in Figure 108 illustrates planetary placements at that time. What stands out on this chart wheel is the T-Square formation with Mars at its apex.

Natal Transits

Events of transiting Sun making 0, 90 and 180 degree aspects to the natal Mars location at 24 Libra have a high propensity to align to pivot swing points. The price chart in Figure 109 illustrates further. A significant price peak and reversal in January 2018 came days ahead of a square aspect. A conjunct aspect in October, 2018 delivered another price peak and reversal. An opposition event and a square event so far in 2019 have resulted in declines of over 1 cent in price.

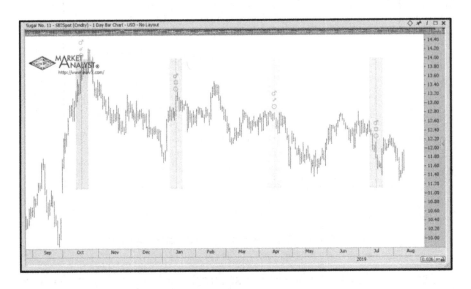

Figure 109
Sugar prices and natal transits

For 2020, transiting Sun will make the following aspects to natal Mars:

90 degrees from January 8 through the 23rd

180 degrees from April 6 through the 23rd

90 degrees from July 9 through the 25th

0 degrees from October 10 through the 26th

Retrograde

Mercury retrograde events have a propensity to align to short term trend changes on Sugar price as the chart in Figure 110 illustrates. Keep your eye on Mercury retrograde events and Sugar trends.

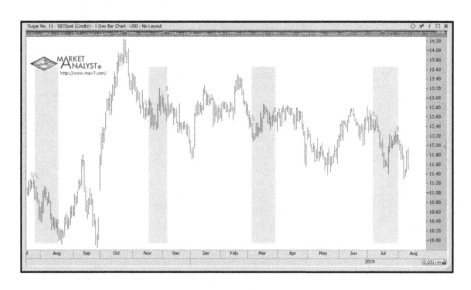

Figure 110
Mercury retrograde and Sugar price

For 2020, Mercury will be:

retrograde from February 17 through March 9.
retrograde from June 18 through July 11.
retrograde from October 14 through November 2.

Cocoa

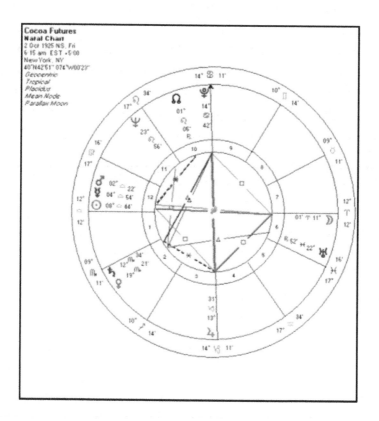

Figure 111
Cocoa futures First Trade horoscope

Cocoa futures started trading in New York in early 1925. The horoscope in Figure 111 shows planetary placements at the first trade date. What I find peculiar on this horoscope wheel is the Mid-Heaven point is located at 14 of Cancer, that same mysterious point that appears in the First Trade horoscope of the New York Stock Exchange.

Retrograde

Mercury retrograde events have a high propensity to align

to pivot swing points on Cocoa price. The price chart in Figure 112 illustrates further. Sometimes a Mercury retrograde event can deliver some erratic volatility as part of an ongoing trend, while other times the retrograde event can bring about a complete change of trend either immediately before the retrograde or immediately after. Either way, Mercury retrograde events deserve close scrutiny.

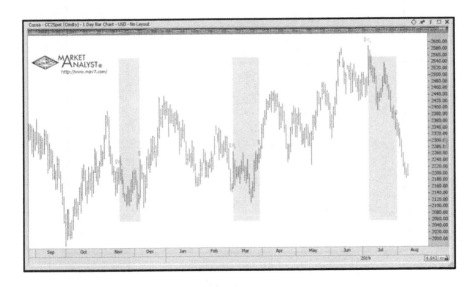

Figure 112
Mercury retrograde and Cocoa price

The alignment to price swing points is very evident in studying Figure 112.

For 2020, Mercury will be:

retrograde from February 17 through March 9.
retrograde from June 18 through July 11.
retrograde from October 14 through November 2.

Conjunctions and Elongations

The 1925 natal horoscope shows Sun and Mercury conjunct (0 degrees apart). My research has shown that events of Mercury being at its maximum easterly and westerly elongations and events of Mercury being at its Inferior and Superior conjunctions align quite well to pivot swing points. The price chart in Figure 113 illustrates both phenomena further. I am particularly intrigued with the East and west elongation alignment to pivot price points.

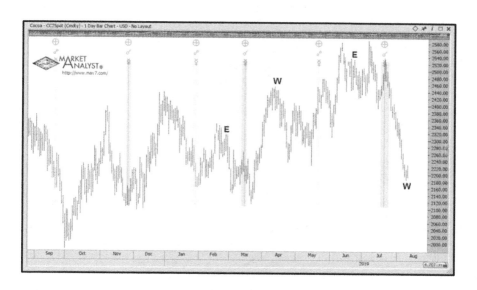

Figure 113
Cocoa price and Mercury cycles

For 2020, Mercury will be at greatest easterly elongation February 10, June 3 and October 1. Greatest westerly elongation will occur March 24, July 22, and November 10.

For 2020, Mercury will be at Inferior Conjunction February 25, June 30, and October 25. Superior

Conjunctions will occur January 10, May 4, August 17 and December 19

CHAPTER TWELVE

Price and Time

Gann Fan Lines

Gann lines are a technique in which a starting point of a significant high or low is selected. From this point, angles (vectors) are projected outwards. These vectors are the 1x1, 1x2, 1x4, 1x8 and the 2x1, 4x1 and 8x1. In and of themselves, these Gann Lines are not related to astrology. However, in my opinion, they should be applied to charts and used in combination with astrology.

Many market data software platforms will come with a Gann Fan function already built in. The confusion with Gann lines comes from the mathematical method of constructing the lines. In fact, in the Market Analyst program there are no fewer than ten ways to apply Gann Lines to a chart. If Mr. Gann were around today he would probably shake his head in bewilderment at how convoluted his technique has become. My preference for apply Gann Lines is the methodology used by Daniel Ferrera in his book Gann for the Active Trader. Ferrera's method is based on the Gann Square of Nine mathematics.

To illustrate the creation of Gann lines, I will use a standard example of Gold prices and this example appears in past Almanacs. Follow the methodology that is described in the following paragraphs and you will soon have Gann Lines on your chart. You do not need a fancy software program to do this. The methodology is as follows:

On March 17, 2014, Gold made a price high at $1392. This is the point from which I wish to extend Gann lines.

Step 1: Take the $1392 and express it simply as the number 1392. Take the square root of the number 1392 and you get 37.3. This will be your time factor.

Step 2: Subtract 1 from 37.3 and re-square this figure to get 1318.

Step 3: We can now state that our time factor is 37.3 calendar days. For simplicity, we can round this off to 37 days. We can further state that our price factor is 1392 minus 1318 = $74.

Step 4: From the March 17 date, extend a line so that it passes through the time co-ordinate (March 17+37 days = April 23) and the price co-ordinate $1318. This line is the Gann 1x1 line.

Step 5: From the March 17 date, extend a line so that it

passes through the time co-ordinate (March 17+(37 x 2) days = May 30) and the price co-ordinate $1318. This line is the Gann 1x2 line.

Step 6: From the March 17 date, extend a line so that it passes through the time co-ordinate ((March 17+(0.5)*37)days = April 4) and the price co-ordinate $1318. This line is the Gann 2x1 line.

Step 7: From the March 17 date, extend a line so that it passes through the time co-ordinate ((March 17+(0.25)*37)days = March 26) and the price co-ordinate $1318. This line is the Gann 4x1 line.

The Gold price chart in Figure 114 has these Gann lines overlaid starting from the March $1392 high.

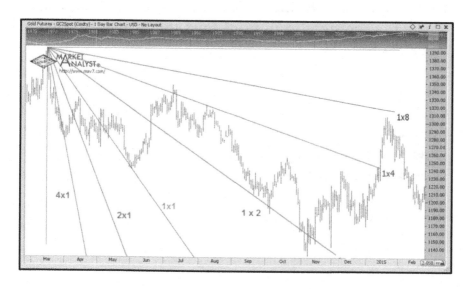

Figure 114
Gann Lines applied to a Gold Chart

This chart has been prepared in the Market Analyst software platform, but as I say you do not necessarily need a fancy software program. A pencil and a ruler could be used to draw lines onto a chart printout.

Notice from the $1392 high, price action dropped, following the 4x1 line. A rally then pushed price up to the 1x1 line. The rally failed and price fell back to the 2x1 line. A sideways consolidation then ensued for several weeks. A price low was registered right at the 1x1 line. Price then rallied up through the 1x2 line and hit resistance at the 1x4 line. Price then drifted lower and eventually recorded a significant low in the November 2014 timeframe just a bit underneath the 1x2 line. In early 2015, a rally failed just shy of the 1x8 line. It is fascinating how these Lines act as support and resistance.

Figure 115 presents a Gold chart with Gann Lines applied from a July 6, 2016 high. Figure 115 also has Gann Lines applied to the significant price lows that were recorded in late 2016.

The downward sloping 1x8 line provided support in late 2017 and again in August 2018. The upward sloping 1x4 line is providing resistance to a rally in February 2018. Now, use this Gann Line chart in combination with the astrological events affecting Gold outlined in the previous chapter and you have a powerful tool at your hands.

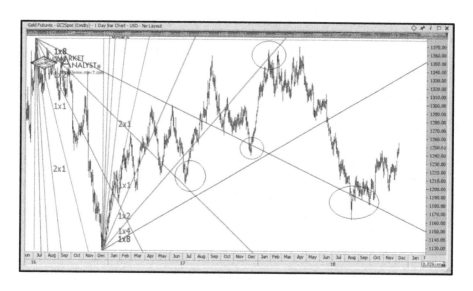

Figure 115
Gann Lines and Gold 2018

To assist you further, I have applied Gann lines to the price low point made in August 2018. This is illustrated in Figure 116.

Figure 116
Gann Lines and Gold 2019

Let's take a look at one more standard example which appears in past Almanacs. Consider the price action of Crude Oil which registered a significant high on June 20, 2014 at $107.73.

Step 1: Take the $107.73 and express it simply as the number 1077.3. Take the square root of the number 1077.3 and you get 32.8. This will be your time factor.

Step 2: Subtract 1 from 32.8 and re-square this figure to get 1011.24.

Step 3: We can now state that our time factor is 33 calendar days. We can further state that our price factor is 1077 minus 1011 = $66.

Step 4: From the June 20 date, you will extend a line so that it passes through the time co-ordinate (June 20 +33 days = July 24) and the price co-ordinate $101.1. This line is the Gann 1x1 line.

Step 5: From the June 20 date, you will extend a line so that it passes through the time co-ordinate (June 20+(33 x 2) days = August 26) and the price co-ordinate $101.1. This line is the Gann 1x2 line.

Next, consider that Crude Oil made a significant low on March 18, 2015 at the $42.30 level.

Step 1: Take the $42.30 level and express it simply as the number 423.0. Take the square root of the number 423.0 and you get 20.56. This will be your time factor.

Step 2: Add 1 to 20.56 and re-square this figure to get 464.83.

Step 3: We can now state that our time factor is 20.56 calendar days. We can further state that our price factor is 464 minus 423 = $41.

Step 4: From the March 18 date, you will extend a line so that it passes through the time co-ordinate (March 18 +20 days = April 8) and the price co-ordinate $46.48. This line is the Gann 1x1 line.

Step 5: From the March 18 date, you will extend a line so that it passes through the time co-ordinate (March 18 + (20 x 2) days = April 28) and the price co-ordinate $46.48. This line is the Gann 1x2 line.

Step 6: From the March 18 date, you will extend a line so that it passes through the time co-ordinate (March 18 + (20 x 8) days = August 29) and the price co-ordinate $46.48. This line is the Gann 1x8 line.

The Crude Oil price chart in Figure 117 has these Gann lines overlaid starting from the June 2014 $107.73 high.

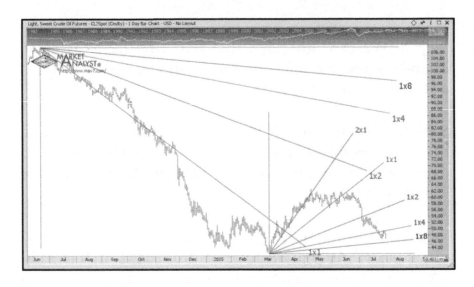

Figure 117
Gann Lines applied to a Crude Oil chart

To bring this Oil example into the current timeframe, recall that Crude made a significant low in late December, 2018. Using this 2018 low, Figure 118 presents a crude Oil price chart overlaid with Gann Lines. For the first several months of 2019, price action followed the 1 x 1 Gann line, More recently, the 1 x 4 line has been providing support as Crude Oil displays weaker price action.

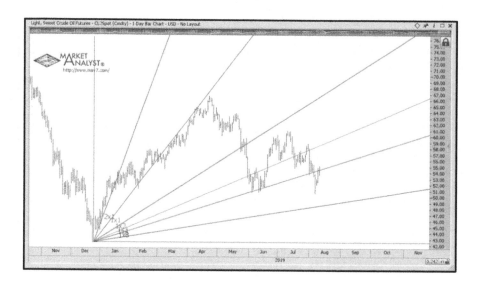

Figure 118 Updated Gann Lines and Crude Oil

Gann Planetary Transit Lines

While on the subject of Gann and Lines, there is one astrological technique whose power continues to amaze me. The technique I refer to is Gann Planetary Transit Lines. (For a detailed description of how to construct Transit Lines, see my second book, *The Lost Science* or see Jeanne Long's book, *The Universal Clock*. The construction methodology is quite simple and either of these publications will step you through it).

Transit lines involve taking the longitudinal position of a given planet and converting that longitude to price by means of the Wheel of 24 (also known as the Universal Clock). Typically, transit lines are plotted for Mars, Jupiter, Saturn, Uranus and Neptune. Once the transit lines have been calculated and plotted, one can then overlay price data on the chart.

Figure 119
Crude Oil and Uranus Transit Lines

Figure 119 illustrates a chart of Crude Oil prices to which I have added the Uranus transit lines with sub-harmonic divisions. This chart has been prepared in the Market Analyst software platform using the built-in Gann Planetary Transit function.

Notice how price high in October 2018 and the low in December 2018 both align to Uranus sub-harmonics. More recently, the trend change in April 2019 also aligned to a Uranus sub-harmonic.

To further illustrate the power of transit lines, consider the chart in Figure 120 of the Dow Jones Industrial Average which has been overlaid with Mars transit lines. Note how these transit lines have frequently aligned to support and resistance levels including the precipitous December 2018 lows.

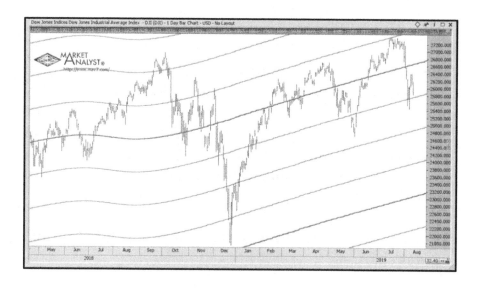

Figure 120
Dow Jones Average and Mars Transit Lines

For readers in Australia, Figure 121 illustrates how the various harmonics of Mars transit lines offer support and resistance to the S&P/ASX 200.

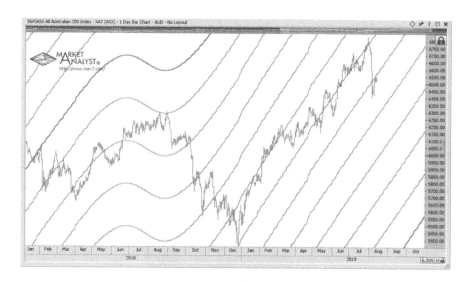

Figure 121
ASX 200 and Jupiter Transit Lines 2019

Price square Time

The concept of *price square time* says that at a significant swing point and trend change on a stock chart, commodity price chart or index chart exists because price and time have squared with one another. That is, a planet has advanced a certain number of degrees and price has changed by that same number of degrees or a multiple of those degrees.

To illustrate, Figure 122 presents a segment from a Gold futures chart.

Price Rise = $187

Figure 122
Gold price and the concept of Price square Time

This chart shows that from August 18 through February 2019 there was a clear uptrend, which broke in February 2019. The price rise from low to high (intraday) was $187.

During this timeframe, Sun advanced 187 degrees (23 Leo to 0 Pisces) and Venus advanced from 8 Libra to 12 Capricorn (94 degrees ; 94 x 2 = 188), Mars moved from 29 Capricorn to 2 Taurus (93 degrees ; 93 x 2 = 186). Mercury and Jupiter moved 210 degrees and 35 degrees respectively – so they are not significant to this argument.

The planetary movement squares (closely matches) the price movement. Identifying price square time events will take some work on your part. But, the results will make the effort worthwhile. When dealing with large price values, such as the Dow Jones, the Nasdaq or the S&P 500, you will end up using a multiplier on the planetary movement values. To illustrate, Figure 123 is a price chart of the Dow Jones Industrial Average.

Figure 123
Dow Jones and the concept of Price square Time

From the early October, 2018 turning point to the December low point, the Dow dropped 3950 points.

During this same time frame, heliocentric Venus moved 132 degrees. If we take 30 times 132 we get 3960 and we can argue that price and time are square.

From the December lows, the Dow sharply recovered, finally hitting a turning point on April 23, 2019. The price move over this timeframe was 3778 points (close to close). During this same time, heliocentric Venus moved 189 degrees. If we take 20 times 189 we get 3780 and we can argue that price and time have squared. I have yet to fully comprehend the mysteries of price squaring with time. Why in one instance does a 20 X multiplier work, when in the other instance a 30 X factor works? Why are these multipliers always whole integer numbers?

If you are prepared to take the time to determine both geocentric and heliocentric movements, price square time will prove to be a powerful tool for you.

Newton and Einstein

In the early 1700s and scientist Sir Isaac Newton developed his theory of Universal Gravitation in which he said planets in our solar system are attracted to one another by gravity. Newton further said that space and time were absolute and that the world functioned according to an absolute order. Furthermore, he said that space was a three-dimensional entity and time was a two-dimensional entity.

In the early 1900's, Albert Einstein advanced his Theory of Relativity that posited Newton's absolute model was outdated. Einstein said the passage of time of an object was related to its speed with respect to that of another observer. Thus was penned the concept of relative space-time in which space was not uniform.

Einstein further stated that relative space-time could be distorted depending on the density of matter. That is, space-time in the area of the Sun is more distorted because the Sun has a great, huge mass. Light particles travelling near the Sun are then distorted from their linear path due to the mass of the Sun.

Quantum Price Lines

Quantum Price Lines are based on this quantum theory. The whole notion of Quantum Lines posits that the price of a stock, index or commodity can be thought of as a light particle or electron that can occupy different energy levels or orbital shells.

Author and market researcher Fabio Oreste has done a masterful job of taking quantum physics, blending it with the curvature mathematics of Riemann and applying the whole thing to price charting. Price is considered to be akin to light particles. These light particles are then deflected by actions of planets. This deflection is what gives us price highs and lows on a chart. Essentially, what Oreste has done is take the Gann Transit Line notion and marry it to modern physics and bring it into the 21st century. Oreste's book is entitled *Quantum Trading* and is available through most on-line book-sellers.

To save you the trouble of buying the book, the Oreste formula for Quantum Price Line calculation is :

Quantum Line = (N x 360) + PSO ;

Where PSO = heliocentric planetary longitude x Conversion Scale
Where N is the harmonic level = 2n ; 1,2,4,8,16 ....
Where Conversion Scale = 2n ; 1,2,4,8,16 ....

When dealing with prices less than 360, the inverse variation of the formula is used.

Quantum Line = (1/N x 360) + PSO

The technique then allows one to calculate various sub-divisions of these Quantum Lines. Taking the value of the calculated Quantum Line, one would generate the sub-divisions by multiplying by 1.0625, 1.125, 1.875, 1.25 etc... in steps of 0.0625.

Please note the use of heliocentric planetary data in these Quantum Line calculations. There are websites that will provide you with this data. One site I use is found at: www.astro.com/swisseph.

Alternatively, you can find a Heliocentric Ephemeris book. The one that I have is entitled: *The American Heliocentric Ephemeris, 2001-2050.*

To go into a lengthy description of Quantum Lines would quickly double the size of this manuscript. In the interest of brevity, what follows is a listing of the Quantum lines you may wish to overlay onto your various charts for 2020. You may be shocked to find how price action tends to closely respect these Lines and sub-divisions thereof.

S&P 500 Index

I have found that the Pluto quantum lines and Neptune Quantum Lines (Conversion Scale =2, N=2) work quite well for the S&P 500 Index. During 2019, consider drawing the following suite of Quantum Lines onto your daily chart of the S&P500 Index. Each line should start at January 1, 2020 and terminate at December 31, 2020.

Pluto - January 2020	Pluto - December 2020
2119	2125
2200	2207
2282	2289
2363	2370
2445	2452
2526	2534
2608	2616
2771	2779
2934	2943
3097	3106
3260	3270
3423	3433
3586	3597
3749	3760

Neptune - January 2020	Neptune - December 2020
2121	2130
2209	2218
2297	2307
2386	2396
2474	2485
2562	2573
2651	2662
2739	2751
2828	2840
3004	3017
3181	3195
3358	3372
3535	3550
3711	3727

Nasdaq Composite Index

I have found that the Pluto quantum lines (Conversion Scale =4, N=8) work quite well for the Nasdaq Composite. During 2019, consider drawing the following suite of Quantum Lines onto your daily chart of the Nasdaq Composite. Each line should start at January 1, 2020 and terminate at December 31, 2020.

January 2020	December 2020
5216	5232
5542	5559
5868	5886
6194	6213
6520	6540
6846	6867
7172	7194
7498	7521
7824	7848
8150	8175
8476	8502
8802	8829
9128	9156

Dow Jones Industrial Average

I have found that the Pluto quantum lines (Conversion Scale =2, N=32) work quite well for the Dow Jones Average. During 2020, consider drawing the following suite of Quantum Lines onto your daily chart of the Dow. Each line should start at January 1, 2020 and terminate at December 31, 2020.

January 2020	December 2020
19560	19620
20212	20274
20864	20928
22168	22236
23472	23544
24776	24852
26080	26160
27384	27468
28688	28776
29992	30084
31296	31392
32600	32700

FTSE 100 Index

I have found that the Pluto Quantum Lines (Conversion Scale =8, N=2) work quite well for the FTSE 100. During 2020, consider drawing the following suite of Quantum Lines onto your daily chart of the FTSE. Each line should start at January 1, 2020 and terminate at December 31, 2020.

January 2020	December 2020
5348	5376
5539	5568
5730	5760
5921	5952
6112	6144
6344	6348
6740	6744
7137	7141
7533	7538
7930	7935
8326	8331

S&P ASX 200 Index

I have found that the Pluto Quantum Lines (Conversion Scale =8, N=2) work quite well for the ASX 200. During 2020, consider drawing the following suite of Quantum Lines onto your daily chart of the ASX 200. Each line should start at January 1, 2020 and terminate at December 31, 2020.

January 2020	December 2020
4966	4992
5157	5184
5348	5376
5539	5568
5730	5760
5921	5952
6112	6144
6344	6348
6740	6744
7137	7141
7533	7538

Gold Futures

I have found that the Pluto Quantum Lines (Conversion Scale=1, N=2) work quite well for Gold. During 2020, consider drawing the following suite of Quantum Lines onto your daily chart of Gold. Each line should start at January 1, 2020 and terminate at December 31, 2020.

January 2020	December 2020
1075	1077
1138	1140
1201	1204
1265	1267
1328	1330
1391	1394
1454	1457
1518	1521
1581	1584
1644	1647
1707	1711
1771	1774
1834	1837
1897	1901
1960	1964

Silver Futures

I have found that the Pluto Quantum Lines (Conversion Scale=1/64 and 1/32, N=1/64 and 1/32) work quite well for Silver. During 2020, consider drawing the following suite of Quantum Lines onto your daily chart of Silver. Each line should start at January 1, 2020 and terminate at December 31, 2020.

January 2020	December 2020
13.37	13.41
14.01	14.05
14.64	14.69
15.28	15.33
15.92	15.97
16.55	16.61
17.19	17.24
17.83	17.88
18.46	18.52
19.10	19.16
19.74	19.80

Currency Futures (Canadian Dollar, Australian Dollar, Japanese Yen)

I have found that the Pluto Quantum Lines (Conversion Scale=1/1024, N=1/1024) work quite well for these currencies. During 2020, consider drawing the following suite of Quantum Lines onto your daily chart of each of these currencies. Each line should start at January 1, 2020 and terminate at December 31, 2020.

January 2020	December 2020
0.6390	0.6409
0.6789	0.6810
0.7188	0.7210
0.7588	0.7611
0.7987	0.8012
0.8386	0.8412
0.8786	0.8813
0.9185	0.9213
0.9584	0.9614
0.9984	1.0014
1.0383	1.0415
1.0782	1.0816
1.1182	1.1216
1.1581	1.1617
1.1981	1.2017
1.2380	1.2418

Currency Futures (Euro and British Pound)

I have found that the Pluto Quantum Lines (Conversion Scale=1/1024 & 1/512, N=1/1024 & 1/512) work quite well for these currencies. During 2020, consider drawing the following suite of Quantum Lines onto your daily chart of each of these currencies. Each line should start at January 1, 2020 and terminate at December 31, 2020.

January 2020	December 2020
1.0347	1.0378
1.0745	1.0778
1.1143	1.1177
1.1541	1.1576
1.1938	1.1975
1.2336	1.2374
1.2734	1.2773
1.3530	1.3572
1.4326	1.4370
1.5122	1.5168
1.5918	1.5967
1.6714	1.6765
1.7510	1.7563
1.8306	1.8362
1.9102	1.9160

Wheat and Corn Futures

I have found that the Pluto Quantum Lines (Conversion Scale=1/256 & 1/128, N=1/256 & 1/128) work quite well for these currencies. During 2020, consider drawing the following suite of Quantum Lines onto your daily chart of each of these grains. Each line should start at January 1, 2020 and terminate at December 31, 2020.

January 2020	December 2020
3.66	3.67
3.82	3.83
3.98	3.99
4.14	4.15
4.30	4.31
4.46	4.47
4.62	4.63
4.78	4.79
4.93	4.95
5.09	5.11
5.41	5.43
5.73	5.75
6.05	6.07
6.37	6.39
6.69	6.71

Soybean Futures

I have found that the Pluto Quantum Lines (Conversion Scale=1/64 & 1/128, N=1/64 & 1/128) work quite well for Beans. During 2020, consider drawing the following suite of Quantum Lines onto your daily chart of Beans. Each line should start at January 1, 2020 and terminate at December 31, 2020.

January 2020	December 2020
7.00	7.03
7.32	7.34
7.64	7.66
7.96	7.98
8.28	8.30
8.60	8.62
8.91	8.94
9.23	9.26
9.55	9.58
9.87	9.90
10.19	10.22
10.82	10.86
11.46	11.50
12.10	12.13

Crude Oil Futures

I have found that the Pluto Quantum Lines (Conversion Scale=1/32, 1/16 N=1/32, 1/16) work quite well for Oil. During 2020, consider drawing the following suite of Quantum Lines onto your daily chart of Oil. Each line should start at January 1, 2020 and terminate at December 31, 2020.

January 2020	December 2020
26.74	26.82
28.02	28.10
29.29	29.38
30.56	30.66
31.84	31.93
33.11	33.21
34.38	34.49
35.66	35.77
36.93	37.04
38.20	38.32
39.48	39.60
40.75	40.88
43.30	43.43
45.84	45.98
48.39	48.54
50.94	51.09
53.48	53.65
56.03	56.20
58.58	58.76
61.13	61.31
63.67	63.87
66.22	66.42
68.77	68.98

30 Year Bond Futures

I have found that the Saturn Quantum Lines (Conversion Scale=1/4 & 1/8, N=1/4 & 1/8) work fairly well for Bonds. During 2020, consider drawing the following suite of Quantum Lines onto your daily chart of Bonds. Each line should start at January 1, 2020 and terminate at December 31, 2020.

January 2020	December 2020
132	134
137	139
142	144
147	149
152	155
157	160
163	165
173	175
183	186
193	196
203	206

10 Year Treasury Note Futures

I have found that the Pluto Quantum Lines (Conversion Scale=1/8, N=1/8) work not too badly for Treasuries. During 2019, consider drawing the following suite of Quantum Lines onto your daily chart of Treasuries. Each line should start at January 1, 2020 and terminate at December 31, 2020.

January 2020	December 2020
106.97	107.30
112.06	112.41
117.16	117.52
122.25	122.63
127.34	127.73
132.44	132.84
137.53	137.95
142.63	143.06

Sugar Futures

I have found that the Pluto quantum lines (Conversion Scale = 1/64 and 1/32). During 2020, consider drawing the following suite of quantum lines onto your daily chart of Sugar prices. Each line should start at January 1, 2020 and terminate at December 31, 2020.

January 2020	December 2020
9.55	9.58
9.87	9.90
10.19	10.22
10.82	10.86
11.46	11.50
12.10	12.13
12.73	12.77
13.37	13.41
14.01	14.05
14.64	14.69
15.28	15.33
15.92	15.97
16.55	16.61
17.19	17.24

Cocoa Futures

I have found that the Pluto Quantum Lines (Conversion Scale=2 N=2) work quite well for Cocoa. During 2020, consider drawing the following suite of Quantum Lines onto your daily chart of Cocoa. Each line should start at January 1, 2020 and terminate at December 31, 2020.

January 2020	December 2020
1793	1798
1874	1880
1956	1962
2037	2043
2119	2125
2200	2207
2282	2289
2363	2370.
2445	2452
2526	2534
2608	2616
2771	2779
2934	2943
3097	3106

CHAPTER THIRTEEN

Conclusion

I have taken you on a wide ranging journey in this almanac to acquaint you with the mathematical and astrological links between investor emotion and market behavior. I sincerely hope you will embrace Financial Astrology as a valuable tool to assist you in your trading and investing activity. I hope you will pause often to reflect on the deeper connection between the financial markets, astrology and the emotions of mankind. And, as unsettling as it may be, I further hope that you pause to reflect on the connection between astrology and the men in dark suits sitting in their wood-panelled offices who may be using it to manipulate the markets.

On that note, I will leave you with the words of Neil Turok from his 2012 book, The Universe Within.

"Perseverance leads to enlightenment. And the truth is more beautiful than your wildest dreams".

CHAPTER FOURTEEN

Glossary of Terms

Ascendant: One of four cardinal points on a horoscope, the Ascendant is situated in the East.

Aspect: The angular relationship between two planets measured in degrees.

Autumnal Equinox: (see Equinox) – That time of year when Sun is at 0 degrees Libra.

Conjunct: An angular relationship of 0 degrees between two planets.

Cosmo-biology: Changes in human emotion caused by changes in cosmic energy.

Descendant: One of four cardinal points on a horoscope, the Descendant is situated in the West.

Ephemeris: A daily tabular compilation of planetary and lunar positions.

Equinox: An event occurring twice annually, an equinox event marks the time when the tilt of the Earth's axis is neither toward or away from the Sun.

First Trade chart: A zodiac chart depicting the positions of the planets at the time a company's stock or a commodity future commenced trading on a recognized financial exchange.

First Trade date: The date a stock or commodity futures contract first began trading on a recognized exchange.

Full Moon: From a vantage point situated on Earth, when the Moon is seen to be 180 degrees to the Sun.

Geocentric Astrology: That version of Astrology in which the vantage point for determining planetary aspects is the Earth.

Heliocentric Astrology: That version of Astrology in which the vantage point for determining planetary aspects is the Sun.

House: A 1/12th portion of the zodiac. Portions are not necessarily equal depending on the mathematical formula used to calculate the divisions.

Lunar Eclipse: A lunar eclipse occurs when the Sun, Earth, and Moon are aligned exactly, or very closely so, with the Earth in the middle. The Earth blocks the Sun's rays from striking the Moon.

Lunar Month: (see Synodic Month).

Lunation: (see New Moon).

Mid-Heaven: One of four cardinal points on a horoscope, the Mid-Heaven is situated in the South.

New Moon: From a vantage point situated on Earth, when the Moon is seen to be 0 degrees to the Sun.

North Node of Moon: The intersection points between the Moon's plane and Earth's ecliptic are termed the North and South nodes. Astrologers tend to focus on the North node and Ephemeris tables clearly list the zodiacal position of the North Node for each calendar day.

Orb: The amount of flexibility or tolerance given to an aspect.

Retrograde motion: The apparent backwards motion of a planet through the zodiac signs when viewed from a vantage point on Earth.

Sidereal Month: The Moon orbits Earth with a slightly elliptical pattern in approximately 27.3 days, relative to a fixed frame of reference.

Sidereal Orbital Period: The time required for a planet to make one full orbit of the Sun as viewed from a fixed vantage point on the Sun.

Siderograph: A mathematical equation developed by astrologer Donald Bradley in 1946 (By plotting the output of the equation against date, inflection points can be seen on the plotted curve. It is at these inflection points that human emotion is most apt to change resulting in a trend change on the Dow Jones or S&P 500 Index).

Solar Eclipse: A solar eclipse occurs when the Moon passes between the Sun and Earth and fully or partially blocks the Sun.

Solstice: Occurring twice annually, a solstice event marks the time when the Sun reaches its highest or lowest altitude above the horizon at noon.

Synodic Month: During a sidereal month (see Sidereal Month), Earth will revolve part way around the Sun thus making the average apparent time between one New Moon and the next New Moon longer than the sidereal month at approximately 29.5 days. This 29.5 day time span is called a Synodic Month or sometimes a Lunar Month.

Synodic Orbital Period: The time required for a planet to make one full orbit of the Sun as viewed from a fixed vantage point on Earth.

Vernal Equinox: That time of the year when Sun is at 0 degrees Aries.

Zodiac: An imaginary band encircling the 360 degrees of the planetary system divided into twelve equal portions of 30 degrees each.

Zodiac Wheel: A circular image broken into 12 portions of 30 degrees each. Each portion represents a different astrological sign.

CHAPTER FIFTEEN

Other Books by the Author

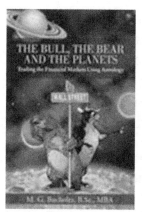

Once maligned by many, the subject of financial Astrology is now experiencing a revival as traders and investors seek deeper insight into the forces that move the financial markets.

The markets are a dynamic entity fueled by many factors, some of which we can easily comprehend, some of which are esoteric. This book introduces the reader to the notion that astrological phenomena can influence price action on financial markets and create trend changes across both short and longer term time horizons. From an introduction to the historical basics behind Astrology through to an examination of lunar Astrology and planetary aspects, the numerous illustrated examples in this book will introduce the reader the power of Astrology and its impact on both equity markets and commodity futures markets.

The financial markets are a reflection of the psychological emotions of traders and investors. These emotions ebb and flow in harmony with the forces of nature.

Scientific techniques and phenomena such as square root mathematics, the Golden Mean, the Golden Sequence, lunar events, planetary transits and planetary aspects have been used by civilizations dating as far back as the ancient Egyptians in order to comprehend the forces of nature.

The emotions of traders and investors can be seen to fluctuate in accordance with these forces of nature. Lunar events can be seen to align with trend changes on financial markets. Significant market cycles can be seen to align with planetary transits and aspects. Price patterns on stocks, commodity futures and market indices can be seen to conform to square root and Golden Mean mathematics.

In the early years of the 20th century the most successful traders on Wall Street, including the venerable W.D. Gann, used these scientific techniques and phenomena to profit from the markets. However, over the ensuing decades as technology has advanced, the science has been lost.

The Lost Science acquaints the reader with an extensive range of astrological and mathematical phenomena. From the Golden Mean and Fibonacci Sequence, to planetary transit lines and square roots through to an examination of lunar Astrology and planetary aspects, the numerous illustrated examples in this book will show the reader how these unique scientific phenomena impact the financial markets.

Very little is known about Louise McWhirter, except that in 1937 she wrote the book McWhirter Theory of Stock Market Forecasting.

In my travels to places as far away as the British Library in London, England to research financial Astrology, not once did I come across any other books by her. Not once did I find any other book from her era that even mentioned her name. All of this I find to be deeply mysterious. Whoever she was – she wrote only one book, and it was a powerful one that is as accurate today as it was back in 1937. The purpose of writing this book is suggested by the title itself – to de-mystify McWhirter's methodology - which is not exactly straightforward.

Can the movements of the Moon affect the stock market?

Are price swings on Crude Oil, Soybeans, the British pound and other financial instruments a reflection of planetary placements?

The answer to these questions is YES. Changes in price trends on the markets are in fact related to our changing emotions. Our emotions in turn are impacted by the changing events in our cosmos.

In the early part of the 20th century many successful traders on Wall Street, including the venerable W.D. Gann and the mysterious Louise McWhirter, understood that emotion was linked to the forces of the cosmos. They used astrological events and esoteric mathematics to predict changes in price trend and to profit from the markets.

However, in the latter part of the 20th century, the investment community has become more comfortable just relying on academic financial theory and the opinions of colorful television media personalities all wrapped up in a buy and hold mentality.

The Cosmic Clock has been written for traders and investors who are seeking to gain an understanding of the cosmic forces that influence emotion and the financial markets.

This book will acquaint you with an extensive range of astrological and mathematical phenomena. From the Golden Mean and Fibonacci Sequence through planetary transit lines, quantum lines, the McWhirter method, planetary conjunctions and market cycles. The numerous illustrated examples in this book will show you how these unique phenomena can deepen your understanding of the financial markets and make you a better trader and investor.

CHAPTER SIXTEEN

About the Author

Malcolm Bucholtz, B.Sc, MBA is a graduate of Queen's University Faculty of Engineering in Canada and Heriot Watt University in Scotland where he received an MBA degree. After working in Canadian industry for far too many years, Malcolm followed his passion for the financial markets by becoming an Investment Advisor/Commodity Trading Advisor with an independent brokerage firm in western Canada. Today, he resides in western Canada where he trades the financial markets using technical chart analysis, esoteric mathematics and the astrological principles outlined in this book.

Malcolm is the author of several books. His first book, *The Bull, the Bear and the Planets,* offers the reader an introduction to Financial Astrology and makes the case that there are esoteric and astrological phenomena that influence the financial markets. His second book, *The Lost Science*, takes the reader on a deeper journey into planetary events and unique mathematical phenomena that influence financial markets. His third book, *De-Mystifying the McWhirter Theory of Stock Market Forecasting* seeks to simplify and illustrate the McWhirter methodology. Malcolm has been writing the *Financial Astrology Almanac* each year since 2014.

Malcolm maintains both a website (www.investingsuccess.ca) where he provides traders and investors with astrological insights into the financial markets. He also offers a monthly *Astrology Letter* service where subscribers receive a bi-weekly previews of pending astrological events that stand to influence markets.

And, if all this were not enough, Malcolm now is pursuing studies towards an M.Sc. degree from Heriot Watt University in his other favorite area of pursuit - Brewing & Distilling.

Recommended Readings

Astrology Really Works, edited by Jill Kramer for The Magi Society,(USA, 1995)

The Bull, the Bear and the Planets, M.G. Bucholtz, (USA, 2013)

The Lost Science, M.G. Bucholtz, (USA, 2013)

Stock Market Forecasting – The McWhirter Method De-Mystified, M.G. Bucholtz, (Canada, 2014)

The Cosmic Clock, M.G. Bucholtz (Canada, 2016)

The Universal Clock, J. Long, (USA, 1995)

McWhirter Theory of Stock Market Forecasting, L. McWhirter, (USA, 1938)

The Universe Within, N. Turok, (Canada, 2012)

A Theory of Continuous Planet Interaction, *NCGR Research Journal,* T.Waterfall, Volume 4, Spring 2014, pp 67-87.

Financial Astrology, Giacomo Albano, (U.K., 2011)

Made in the USA
Coppell, TX
11 March 2020